W9-DDP-552

food adventures

food adventures

introducing your child to
flavors from around
the world

Elisabeth Luard & Frances Boswell

photography by Ngoc Minh Ngo

KYLE BOOKS

For Jessie, Bonnie, Sophie, Harper,
Beatriz Plum, Iona, and Little Brother Orin,
without whom there would have been no book.

This edition published in 2006 by Kyle Books
An imprint of Kyle Cathie Limited
general.enquiries@kyle-cathie.com
www.kylecathie.com

Distributed by National Book Network
4501 Forbes Blvd., Suite 200
Lanham, MD 20706
Phone: (301) 459 3366   Fax: (301) 429 5746

ISBN (10-digit) 1-904920-45-4
ISBN (13-digit) 978-1-904920-45-8

10 9 8 7 6 5 4 3 2 1

Project editor CAROLINE TAGGART
Copy editor MORAG LYALL
Index by ANNA NORMAN
Production by SHA HUXTABLE and ALICE HOLLOWAY
Americanization by DELORA JONES

Printed in Singapore by Star Standard

Ten fingers, ten toes. Check. New life on the planet.

The arrival of a first baby is the moment of truth in any adult relationship. Anyone can fall in love, marry or not. But a baby is something else. It's a joy, naturally, and a responsibility. But it's also earth-shattering, the bolt of lightning which changes the world for ever.

New life needs to eat. And the choice is yours. But all over the world, people who live in multi-generational households don't reach for the package or open the jar. Instead, they feed their babies a little of what they themselves eat, in easily digested form—a practice made possible because someone else is helping around the house. Few of us have such luxury. But most of us do have times—weekends, holidays, even weekday evenings—when cooking is perfectly possible. The aim of this book is to make those times a pleasure rather than a chore.

As members of an extended family, Frances and I—daughter-in-law and mother-in-law—are aware of how much we need each other, trading advice, support, and even, at times, trans-Atlantic babysitting. Happily, we share

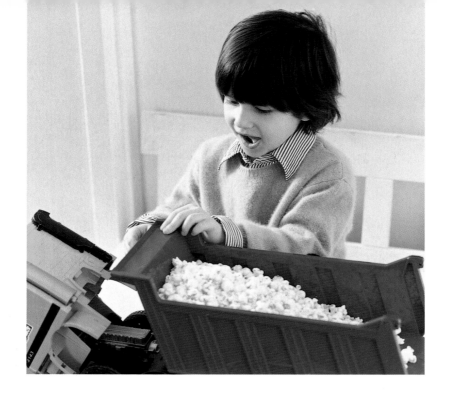

an interest—more than that, a career, since it's the way we both earn our living. We write about food: how it looks, where it comes from, how to make it taste good. Which is not to say we live our lives in exactly the same way. We cook differently, just as we parent differently, and our relationship is all the more valuable because we learn from each other. One of us is naturally innovative, unafraid to substitute an ingredient or present a dish in a new way; the other is instinctively traditional, always looking for the story behind the story, needing to know exactly why the cooks of Portugal have a taste for fresh coriander leaves (cilantro) or the Chinese serve sweet things along with the soup. No prizes for guessing which is which. But we never disagree on

the basics: that food should taste good because it *is* good, and that this is a lesson you're never too young to learn.

Our testers, the dedicatees of this book—their ages ranging from 3 months to 7 years old—didn't like everything we put in front of them. By no means. But they did try everything at least once. And it certainly helped that we knew the food tasted delicious, because we'd tried it ourselves, applying the same standards as we would to any dish we cooked for friends and family. Our children's relationship with food is important to both of us, just as food is important in our relationship with each other.

All the recipes in this book are what the inhabitants of at least one corner of the world consider a normal, healthy diet for their youngsters. None of them will seem more than a little bit exotic since most are familiar if not from travel, then from restaurant menus. Ingredients are mostly what can be picked up at your local store; if they're not we take care to suggest alternatives.

So here we are. The fire's lit. The door's open. Come right in and make yourselves at home.

ELISABETH LUARD
MAY 2006

Frances says: At around 6 months your pediatrician will probably say it is time for something a bit more substantial than milk. Heaven to your ears, and to your bleary eyes, for we all trust that a baby with a full tummy is bound to sleep the night. Packaged cereals are easy, widely available, and come with full nutritional information, perhaps all the baby needs. But they don't do much for the taste buds. And good, nutritious first foods are easily homemade.

first real food
purees and spoonfoods

Elisabeth says: First food is something on a spoon soft enough to be swallowed without chewing—a little taste of what's around, easy to make, and won't upset delicate digestions. From mashed peas to stewed apple to rice pudding, every region has a different notion of what this should be. Your baby doesn't yet have a firm notion of what should be on the spoon—as long as it tastes good, that's fine.

1.a

blueberry soup

Scandinavians and Eastern Europeans love a fruit soup as an appetizer: for grown-ups, chill and top with a spoonful of sour cream and a turn of the pepper mill. Hungary likes its fruit soups made with sour cherries, Romanians prefer apricots, and the Danes favor a mixture of red berries.

Makes about 3 cups
Suitable for 6 months
onwards

9 ounces (about 1½ cups)
ripe blueberries
2 cups spring water
1 level tablespoon cornstarch or
ground rice or potato starch

Blueberries are the most suitable for babies as they don't need sweetening. They are also high in vitamin C and contain a natural enzyme that allows them to keep for a long time in the fridge.

Put the fruit into a saucepan with the spring water. Bring to a boil, reduce the heat, and cook gently until the berries pop and the juices run—5–10 minutes. Strain, mashing to extract all the juice.

Meanwhile, blend the cornstarch or ground rice or potato starch by working it with 1 tablespoon water until runny and free of lumps.

Return the juice to the pan and stir in the cornstarch. Cook until it thickens—5–10 minutes (ground rice takes longer than cornstarch or potato starch)—stirring throughout. Let it cool to finger temperature or chill—teething babies find cold food comforting for sore gums.

leek puree

A spoonful of well-cooked leeks mashed with a little potato is traditionally the first food a Belgian baby tastes, even though members of the onion and garlic tribe are not generally considered suitable for babies. Leeks are traditionally valued for the same virtues as garlic: they are anti-fungal, antibiotic, and generally good for the health. Even more to the point, they once were the only fresh vegetables available when winter was just about to turn to spring—the right time for humans as well as every other mammal to be born.

Makes about 2½ cups
Suitable for 6 months
onwards

1 fine fat leek, white part only,
sliced into fine rings
1 medium potato, peeled and
chopped spring water

Simmer the vegetables in just enough spring water to cover until very tender—30–40 minutes. Drain and mash thoroughly, or push through a food mill (that useful sieving instrument which looks like a drum with a wind-up handle) or blitz in the food processor with enough of the cooking water to make a spoonable puree.

Clockwise from top
left: bluebery soup,
leek puree, rice
congee

rice congee

Rice is the daily bread of China and the rice-growing regions of Southeast Asia, and congee, an unseasoned and unsweetened rice pudding, is eaten much like a slice of toast—for breakfast and as a filler between meals. Light and digestible, it's the perfect baby food. Grownups eat it hot; for babies, let it cool to finger temperature. Indonesian rice expert Sri Owen says her grandmother always made her eat a bowlful of congee when she was under the weather. In Malaysia, baby rice is blended with a taste of salt-cured anchovy—a little extra salt is considered advisable in the tropics, where the body loses salt through the sweat glands.

All rice, even the rice labeled 'glutinous,' is gluten-free, making it non-allergenic. It's also free of extrinsic sugar, the sticky stuff which leads to tooth decay.

If you have time, soak the rice for 2 hours in plenty of cold water, then drain. If not, no matter. Put the rice in a roomy pot and add the water (proportions matter: for a rice to make a pudding, the grains must absorb 4 times their own volume of liquid). Bring to a boil, reduce the heat, loosely cover, and simmer gently for at least 30 minutes, stirring occasionally, until you have a soft, soupy pudding. It freezes well —just pop a supply in the ice-cube tray and defrost a portion as needed.

Makes about 2 cups
Suitable for 6 months onwards

½ cup short-grain rice
(Thai fragrant is perfect)
2½ cups spring water

junket

Soft and slithery, the simplest and most digestible of milk foods—Miss Muffet's curds and whey—junket is all about texture. It's the first stage in the cheese-making process, the result of "turning" (stirring) fresh milk with rennet, a digestive substance found in the stomach lining of all milk-producing animals.

Vegetarian rennet—the substance that transforms milk into curds and whey—is found in a variety of plants, including fig trees, thistles (artichokes, cardoons), and members of the fly-trap family, insect-eating plants which, naturally enough, are equipped with digestive enzymes. Isn't nature wonderful?

Warm the milk to blood temperature, which is the natural heat of the milk when fresh from the cow. Stir in the rennet and sugar and let it set at room temperature: it'll take a couple of hours to turn to soft curds.

Makes 2 cups
Suitable for 6 months onwards

2 cups fresh whole milk
I teaspoon rennet (from the
health food store)
I tablespoon unprocessed
sugar (optional)

apple puree

Climates which are sometimes chilly—Britain, Scandinavia, North America, New Zealand, and southern Australia—are best for apple-growing, and mashed apple is the traditional first food throughout these regions.

Apples are one of a select group of "superfoods" recommended by nutritionists as particularly helpful for promoting good health: great vitamin C as well as satisfying those early hunger pangs.

Make sure the apples are well scrubbed to get rid of any trace of chemicals to which even organics are not entirely immune: include the skin because even if you strain it out this means that all the vitamins concentrated near the surface are not lost.

Pack the apple quarters into a small saucepan, add the water, tightly cover, and cook for 10 minutes, until the apple flesh is perfectly soft. Mash with a fork and push through a strainer or food mill, leaving the skin behind.

Makes about 1 cup
Suitable for 6 months onwards

4 ripe organic eating apples, washed, quartered, and cored
2 tablespoons spring water

pea puree

Peas are the first fresh vegetables of summer, doubly welcome in the cold lands of the north: a soft digestible mash of green peas, the basic ingredient for Denmark's favorite pea soup with dumplings, is the first real food a Danish baby is likely to taste. Danish households have a tradition of careful husbandry and wouldn't want to waste the pods if these were young and tender. If you've bought peas in the pod, drop the empty pods (well-rinsed) on top of the peas to cook in the steam, then scrape out the soft insides to mix with the puree.

Put the shelled peas in a small pan with enough spring water to cover them, bring to a boil, tightly cover, and cook for 2 minutes to soften the skins, then remove the pan from the heat. Pop the peas and their cooking water into the blender and give it a whizz. Then strain—the skins are too hard for a baby's digestion. Or push the peas and their water through a potato-ricer or food mill.

Makes 1 cup
Suitable for 6 months onwards

8 ounces fresh peas in their pods or frozen peas
spring water

Peas are an excellent source of vitamin C, B vitamins, protein, and fiber. Freezing scarcely alters their nutritional value at all.

sweet potato puree

Sweet potato, also known as yam, can be orange-fleshed or ivory-white, though color is no particular indication of sweetness. The sweetest is boniato, a white-fleshed variety popular in Cuba.

Sweet potatoes provide tummy-satisfying starch as well as a chill-beating vitamin C. But they're not advised for windy babies, say West Indian cooks.

Orange-fleshed varieties are rich in beta-carotene, the stuff which turns flamingo feathers pink and, if eaten all the time, gives babies a ruddy glow. If your baby seems to have acquired a golden tan, lay off the orange-colored food.

Makes 2 cups
Suitable for 6 months onwards

1 pound sweet potatoes

Peel the potatoes, chunk into bite-sized pieces, and put in a pan with enough boiling water to cover. Return the water to a boil, reduce the heat, loosely cover and cook for 20–30 minutes, until perfectly soft and tender. Drain—not too thoroughly—reserving a little of the cooking water. Mash to a puree with a little of the cooking water.

Clockwise from top left: apple puree, sweet potato puree, pea puree

Frances says: Combinations—foods which together taste good—push the eating experience one stage further. As both you and your baby grow more confident with the bowl and spoon, eating, like all the best things in life, becomes a happy adventure: what *is* that nutty flavor I detect in my squash? You don't know what your kids will like till they try it—and right now they're not capable of being picky.

first real food
bowl food

Elisabeth says: Every region has its own ideas on combinations that work well together and there's no substitute for traditional knowledge at the family level. Balancing flavor and nutritional value comes naturally when you're preparing foodstuffs familiar from your own childhood. Make it easy by introducing new flavors along with the old: mix, matching something you know they like with something they haven't yet tried.

1.b

polenta with yogurt

A cornmeal pudding as they like it in Romania where, as *mamaliga*, it takes the place of bread on the rural table and is always eaten on its own, as a separate course. For children it's combined with something milky—freshly made curd cheese or yogurt or sour cream—adding protein and a touch of sharpness to balance the natural sweetness.

Cornmeal is a suitable grain food for anyone with a wheat intolerance.

Put the cold spring water into a pan and stir in the cornmeal. Bring to a boil, keeping the heat high until the mixture belches and bubbles. Then turn it down and keep stirring as it thickens and ceases to be grainy—30–40 minutes should see it ready. You can of course make the mixture thicker or thinner as you please just by adding less or more water (if you add water during the cooking, make sure the water's boiling). Remove from the heat and let cool to finger heat; it'll firm as it sets. Finish with the yogurt, stirred in or separate, as you please.

Makes about 2 cups
Suitable for 9 months onwards

3 cups spring water
1 cup fine-ground cornmeal (polenta)
1–2 tablespoons plain yogurt

quinoa and butternut squash

The nutty flavor and grainy texture of quinoa (pronounced *keen-wa*) is delicious with the sweet juicy flesh of one of the squashes, a combination popular in Peru, home territory of both ingredients. Quinoa was the staple grain food of the Incas of Peru—they called it the mother seed. Modern chemists identify it as being remarkably high in protein—particularly lysine, which is difficult to obtain from any other vegetable source. It also supplies fiber, vitamins B and E, calcium, iron, magnesium, and phosphorus.

Put the quinoa grains in a small pan with enough spring water to cover by about 2cm. Bring to a boil, reduce the heat, and simmer for 15–20 minutes until the dark skins pop open, showing the pale insides.

Meanwhile, peel the squash with a sharp knife, remove the fibers and seeds in the middle (discard the fibers, but save the seeds as a nibble—there's a nutty little heart inside) and cut up the flesh. Stir the cut-up squash into the quinoa, let it bubble up, reduce the heat to a gentle simmer, tightly cover, and cook for 20–25 minutes, until the grains are tender and translucent and the squash is completely soft.

Makes about 3 cups
Suitable for 9 months onwards

½ cup quinoa
spring water
1-pound piece butternut or other yellow-fleshed squash

bread and tomato

Every country-bred Italian remembers *papa al pomodoro* as a staple of childhood. Choose perfectly ripe tomatoes and good bread—the kind that weighs heavy in the hand and dries out as it ages—and prepare the dish only when you need it.

Makes about 1 cup
Suitable for 9 months
onwards

1 thick slice dried-out
country bread
1 large field-ripened tomato
½ tablespoon mild olive oil

Tuscan bread is unsalted: perfect for babies. Tomatoes are high in antioxidants, rich in vitamins C and E, and are classed by nutritionists as "superfoods"—foods that are particularly good for health.

Tear the bread into little bits. Cut the tomato in half through the equator and, gripping the skin side of one half firmly in your fist, grate the flesh along with the seeds and juices through the large holes of a cheese grater, leaving you with a scraped-out half moon of skin. Repeat with the other half. Push the resulting pulp through a strainer into a bowl. Stir in the torn bread. Add enough boiling water to soften everything to a pulp. Fork it over gently and leave for 10 minutes for the bread and juices to mix. Trickle with the oil and fork it over again.

red lentils with spinach

The perfect combination: soft-cooked Indian lentils with fresh spinach, a popular dish at the traditional family meal taken after the work day is over. Hindu households—vegetarian by tradition for religious reasons—are particularly good at combining legumes from the cupboard with fresh leafy greens.

Lentils are good for vegetarians or anyone on a low-meat diet since they're rich in protein and deliver a good supply of iron and B vitamins. Legume vegetables, lentils included, are the perfect health food. For babies, cook them a little longer than usual to make them more digestible.

Pick over the lentils, checking for any tiny stones, and put them in a small pan with double their own volume of spring water. Bring to a boil, skim off any foam, reduce the heat, loosely cover, and cook for 30–40 minutes, until the lentils have soaked up most of the water and are soupy and soft; add more boiling water if necessary.

Meanwhile cook the spinach in a little spring water—a spoonful should be enough—in a tightly-lidded pan for 4–5 minutes, until the leaves wilt. Drain the cooking juice into the lentils and chop the leaves very thoroughly (or puree in a blender). Combine the spinach with the lentils and let cool to finger temperature.

Makes about 2 cups
Suitable from 12 months
onwards

¼ cup red or yellow lentils
spring water
2 large handfuls spinach leaves,
picked over and well rinsed

**Prune compote,
potatoes and carrots,
and chicken soup
with rice**

Frances says: Next thing you know, your baby's in a bit of tummy trouble: scarlet-faced with constipation, heaven knows why; or turned bright orange because that's what happens when a person eats nothing but carrot and pumpkin; or broken out in a rash because something didn't agree with the system. Often it's just a matter of making minor adjustments to the diet. Here are some of the first-aid foods which worked for me.

first real food
first aid

Elisabeth says: When my children were growing up in the wilds of Andalusia, our neighbors, subsistence farmers, never consulted a doctor except as a matter of life or death. Camomile tea was taken for a fever; honey applied as a poultice for chicken-pox sores and insect stings. Home remedies are strictly for minor problems, no more than first aid—though that, if fortune is with you, is often all you need.

1.c

prune compote

Makes about 1 cup
Suitable for 9 months onwards

1 cup ready-to-eat organic
prunes, pitted
spring water

What goes in must come out, preferably without having to try too hard. Prunes work on the digestive system by delivering a natural laxative which stimulates the bowel. They're also a good source of iron in easily assimilable form. For extra soothe-power, stir in a spoonful of yogurt.

Put the prunes in a small pan with enough spring water to submerge them. Bring to a boil, reduce the heat, and simmer for about 15 minutes, until the prunes are completely pulpy. Blend with the cooking liquid and, for younger babies, strain it.

potatoes and carrots

Makes about 2½ cups
Suitable for 9 months onwards

about 1 cup peeled,
chopped potato
about 1 cup scraped,
chopped carrot
spring water

This is the Turkish fixer for a runny tummy—it works by acting as a stomach-liner, which is about all anyone can hope for right now.

Rinse the vegetables and put them in a saucepan with enough cold spring water to cover. Bring to a boil, reduce the heat, and simmer for 15–20 minutes, until both vegetables are perfectly tender. Mash them with a little of the cooking water and serve as much as your baby will eat.

chicken soup with rice

Makes about 2 cups
Suitable for 9 months
onwards

1 pound bony chicken bits
(wing-tips, back, neck)
1 large carrot, scraped and
cut into chunks
green tops of 1–2 leeks or
1 onion, quartered
4 cups spring water
½ cup white rice

Whatever the reason—convalescence, sudden discovery of an allergy, loss of appetite—there's always a moment for back-to-basics. Rice cooked in home-made chicken broth—the Mediterranean cure-all—fits the bill. Make it with organically reared, free-range chicken bits.

Rinse the chicken bits and the vegetables and put them in a roomy pot with the spring water. Bring to a boil, allow the water a single belch, and skim off the gray foam that rises. Reduce the heat and simmer gently for 30–40 minutes, until well flavored and reduced by half. Strain, discarding the solids, blot the surface of the soup with paper towels to remove any traces of fat. Let cool, and store in the fridge for no longer than a week. To keep for longer, freeze in ice-cube trays.

Measure 1 1/4 cups of the broth into a small pan and add the rice. Bring to a boil, stir, reduce the heat, and simmer for 30 minutes, till the rice is perfectly soft and tender.

lemon barley water

An old-fashioned homemade recipe, familiar in its commercial form. But the mass-produced barley water contains E-numbers—your own will not.

Popular in rural Britain, particularly in Scotland (where adults take it with honey and a tot of whisky); this version comes from southern Spain, a straight-from-the-cupboard remedy from the hills of Andalucia.

Lemon disinfects, sugar comforts, and barley broth soothes—just what you need when your baby is feeling under the weather.

Drain the barley and put it in a roomy pan with the lemon zest and spring water. Bring to a boil, reduce the heat, loosely cover, and simmer gently for 30–40 minutes, until the barley is soft and the cooking broth is milky and lightly thickened. Strain out the solids and return the broth to the pan.

Stir in the sugar and heat gently, stirring with a wooden spoon until the granules are dissolved. Remove from the heat and stir in the lemon juice.

Dilute to taste—drink it warm in winter and chilled in summer—or administer it undiluted by the spoonful as a soother for a cough or sore throat. You can bottle it up and keep it in the fridge for no longer than a week or freeze it so you have some ready in an emergency.

Makes about 2 cups
Suitable for 9 months onwards

1 tablespoon barley, soaked
  for 2–3 hours or overnight
finely pared zest and juice of
  1 lemon
2 cups spring water
2 tablespoons unbleached sugar

garlic broth

This is a general cure-all and stomach-settler for babies and young children throughout the lands of the Mediterranean, though this particular version is from Provence.

The brew is also good for indigestion and general discomfort when you're pregnant. Garlic, say modern chemists, is antibiotic and antifungal—which might explain why it figures in fairytales as a defense against witches and other undesirables, particularly vampires and things that go bump in the night.

Simmer the garlic and oil in the spring water for 30 minutes. Five minutes before the end of the cooking, add the sage: it'll give the soup a delicate amber tinge and a wonderfully medicinal fragrance. Season with a little salt. For older children and convalescents, stir in a handful of vermicelli—they'll only take 2–3 minutes to cook—and whisk in an egg yolk after you remove the broth from the heat.

Makes about 2 cups
Suitable for 9 months onwards

6 garlic cloves, skinned
   and crushed
2 tablespoons olive oil
2 cups spring water
1 sprig of sage
½ teaspoon salt

mangu

This is a smooth porridge made with mashed cooked plantain, the remedy for an upset tummy in the Dominican Republic and throughout the Caribbean. Plantain, botanically identical to the banana though it never ripens to full softness and sweetness, is one of the most important starch vegetables of the region. The purpose-bred varieties are inedibly bitter when raw; when cooked, they're starchy and bland, and are grown as a staple food in the tropics where grain does not thrive.

Skin the plantains with a very sharp knife—the skin is very firmly attached to the flesh, chop roughly, and cook in boiling water. Alternatively, bake at 450°F for 20–30 minutes till cooked right through, then split down the middle with a sharp knife and scoop out the flesh. Mash thoroughly.

Makes about 1 cup
Suitable for 9 months onwards

2 ripe plantains or green bananas

All members of the banana and plantain family are high in fiber, vitamins, and minerals, particularly potassium.

Frances says: As with most things in kids' lives, parents set the tone. Kids are picky eaters as long as parents let them be. When you say that your toddler won't eat anything except white bread, the reality is that you, the parent, cannot tolerate the storm. But you have more control than you think. Replace the white bread with something good, cut into small bits—not too daunting, not too overwhelming—just so you both know they can do it.

window of opportunity

Elisabeth says: There's an explanation for the window of opportunity. It happens when a baby becomes a toddler, no longer dependent on mother for milk, but not yet able to stray too far. Take advantage while it lasts: once independence is established, every unknown food is likely to be rejected, in case it is poisonous. Practical, really. The more we learn to trust our taste buds when we're young, the more adventurous we'll be as we grow up.

2

patterns

Appeal to your child's sense of wonder by presenting combinations of foods in their unchanged state, as close to natural as possible, which not only taste good together but also look beautiful at first sight.

Encourage appreciation by setting up a pretty tasting-menu—what four-year-old Sophie calls "patrons"—choosing for looks as well as taste. At this early stage, when a child is tasting almost everything edible it encounters for the first time, it makes sense for everyone to make the best of it. Beautiful presentation isn't cheating: successful restaurateurs do it all the time. A chef's reputation rests on his or her ability to transform perfectly ordinary ingredients into something more appealing than the customer could make at home: a dish people are willing to pay for. Presentation—artistry on a plate—ensures a good appetite, promising that the food will taste as good as it looks.

How you achieve this is up to you. Here are a few of the more obvious choices:

- slices of red-skinned apple stacked with slivers of yellow cheese
- orange segments or dried apricots sandwiched with squares of dark chocolate
- slivers of fresh peach with salty, dry-cured ham—prosciutto or serrano
- slices of plain-cooked new potatoes with scraps of crispy bacon
- tomato with mozzarella

Combinations are whatever suits the season and your purse. Just do it together and have fun.

lima beans with greens
limeños con espinacas

Butter beans or limas, Chile's native beans, are the largest and most delicate of the haricot bean tribe. This is a creamy bean soup finished with greens which won't be overwhelmed by the flavor of the plain-cooked beans. Choose a mixture of salad greens—arugula, watercress, mustard greens, baby spinach, mizuna. Haricot beans are inclined to produce flatulence, an indicator that they're rather troublesome to digest. To avoid this problem, babies younger than twelve months can be given a little taste of the cooking broth.

Drain the beans and put them in a roomy pot with the water, garlic, and bay leaf. Bring to a rolling boil, reduce the heat, loosely cover, and let it bubble gently for at least an hour, until perfectly tender, adding more boiling water if necessary. Don't let the pot come off the boil until the beans are tender; how long they take depends upon how long they've been in store—allow 1–1 1/2 hours. Stir in the olive oil, bring back to a boil, and let it bubble for another 3–4 minutes, until the broth thickens a little as it combines with the oil. Offer the greens separately for people to choose which they'd like to stir into the hot broth.

**Purpose: to get to know and
love your greens**
Makes about 4 cups

¾ cup dried butter beans or lima
beans, soaked for 3–4 hours
2½ cups spring water
2–3 garlic cloves, unskinned
1 bay leaf
1–2 tablespoons olive oil
a large handful of mixed
greens, shredded

olives, ham, cheese

Small children love salty things, and nothing is saltier than olives, ham, and cheese, the staples of the Mediterranean larder. Needing no preparation, such foods are eaten as between-meal snacks as well as providing something good to nibble while waiting for dinner. No Italian meal is complete without its antipasto; French children expect an hors d'oeuvre to be provided at every meal, even in school; while in Spain tapas take the place of a formal first course. These habits are acquired young and learned by example, since the pace of life in the lands of the warm south is traditionally more leisurely than that of busy northerners, and families eat together most days—or at least at weekends. At this stage, kids'll try anything as long as they don't have to sit in the highchair and as long as whatever it is looks interesting and can be eaten with the fingers.

Mediterranean parents allow their children to eat moderate amounts of salt-preserved foods, taking care to ensure their charges eat bread with their nibbles, and drink plenty of water to counter the saltiness. Within reason, babies need to replace salt lost to perspiration in centrally heated homes as well as in hot climates.

The difference between getting your salt quota from commercially prepared snack foods and eating traditional nibbles such as olives and artisan cheese is that behind the saltiness are far more complex flavors, opening up the taste buds to a thousand new experiences. There are still hundreds of different regional cheeses made around the shores of the Mediterranean, each as individual as its maker, and just as many varieties of hams and cured sausages; as for olives—well, the infant palate can be given a miniature tour of all the world's flavors without having to leave home. Such foods are also seen as therapeutic. Italian babies are given a pared-down strip of Parmesan rind as a teething ring; Spanish babies get a chewy little strip of serrano ham to soothe sore gums. And the French, aware of their responsibilities as the gourmets of Europe, see an appreciation of cheese as essential equipment for life: it's not too much for a baby to expect a little taste of Roquefort once a week from six months old onwards—not, as you might suppose, to encourage the infant internal flora, but *pour le goût*, so that the child gets the taste.

artichokes with oil and lemon
anginares ladolemono

Purpose: to learn to use
fingers as a precise eating
tool, exploring variations
of taste and texture in the
same foodstuff
Serves 2 children and 2 adults

4 regular-sized artichokes
sea salt

For serving
1 lemon, quartered
about 1 cup olive oil

The presence of cynarin,
a chemical compound said
to improve liver function,
makes artichokes good for
grown-ups who drink wine.
Liver problems make people
bad-tempered—which does
no one any good.

Greek children learn how to dismember an artichoke, the first pleasure of Aegean springtime, very early in their life. It helps to know that the artichoke is a thistle, a member of the daisy family, with green petals ringing around a spiky heart which has to be removed before you can eat the base. You can eat the stalks as well if you strip off the stringy outside; just pop them in the pot along with the artichokes. Children can manage a whole artichoke by themselves: no matter if they don't eat it all—this is an adventure.

Trim the artichokes down to the base of the stalk and remove the small leaves at the base. Don't worry about the prickly ends, they soften in the cooking. And there's no need to rub the cut surfaces with lemon to avoid discoloration if you're going to cook them right away.

Pop the trimmed artichokes into a large pot of lightly salted boiling water. Return the water to a boil and cook the artichokes until tender (about 20–30 minutes depending upon size). Test for doneness by pulling away one of the outer leaves, which should come free quite easily. Drain the artichokes upside-down in a colander so the hot water doesn't stay trapped between the leaves.

When the artichokes have cooled enough to handle comfortably, serve with the lemon quarters and a small cruet of olive oil so everyone can make their own little dipping sauce, *ladolemono*, by mixing the oil and lemon juice to their taste. Grown-ups usually like 2 parts oil to 1 part juice. Salt is an optional extra, and you can replace the lemon juice with vinegar if you prefer.

Alternatively, whisk the lemon juice and the oil together in a small cruet for a ready-made dipping sauce, and provide everyone with an artichoke and a little bowl for the sauce. Set a plate in the middle of the table for the debris.

frittered calamares
calamares a la romana

Purpose: to explore fishy
and chewy food
Serves 2 children and 2 adults

**1 pound ready-cleaned squid,
sliced into rings
2 tablespoons bread flour
light olive oil for shallow-frying**

After handling fish,
rinse your hands in cold water and
they'll never smell fishy. Magic.

The cephalopods—squid (*calamar*), cuttlefish, octopus—are all about texture: the flavor is delicate and sweet, the mouth-feel firm and chewy. In this Spanish dish, given a light dusting of flour and dunked in hot oil for no more than 2–3 minutes, they're a bit like french fries.

Rinse the squid in a strainer under cold water, leaving them damp. Dust with flour (no salt—salting toughens the flesh) and shake vigorously over the sink to allow excess flour to drop through the holes.

Meanwhile, heat a depth of about 2cm olive oil in a frying pan until lightly hazed with blue. Test with a cube of bread: if bubbles form around the edge immediately, it's ready to fry—if the bread browns within seconds, the oil's too hot and should be allowed to cool a little.

Separate the squid rings with your fingers and drop them into the oil only a few at a time to avoid lowering the temperature. Remove with a slotted spoon as soon the flesh turns opaque—don't overcook or it will toughen—and transfer to paper towels.

Continue until all are done. Let cool a little so no one burns their fingers. A squeeze of lemon will cut the richness.

asparagus with eggs
asparagi al uovo

Asparagus is easy to handle and fun to eat, particularly with a dipping sauce of hard-boiled egg mashed up with olive oil, which is the way they like it in Udine, in northern Italy, where they grow early asparagus for the markets of Austria and Germany.

Bring the eggs up to room temperature before you begin. Place them in a small pan with enough cold water to submerge them completely. Bring the water to a boil, reduce the heat to a robust simmer, and cook for 6 minutes—no more. Remove the eggs with a slotted spoon and run cold water over them for a minute to stop the cooking process and loosen the shells ready for peeling.

Wash and trim the asparagus, removing the dry ends and peeling off any tough skin.

Bring a panful of lightly salted water to a boil in a tall narrow pan which will accommodate the asparagus vertically, or lay the spears in a deep wide pan, cover with boiling water, add a little salt, and bring to a boil. Cook for 6–10 minutes, depending upon the thickness of the spears, until the tips are tender but the stalks not yet floppy. Drain carefully and let cool to finger temperature.

Serve each person with a few spears of asparagus, a shelled egg for mashing, and enough oil to make a dipping sauce. Provide sea salt or not, as you please.

Purpose: to explore mouthfeel, combining sauce ingredients to suit yourself
Serves 2 children and 2 adults

1 pound fresh asparagus spears
sea salt

For serving
4 organic cage-free eggs, hard-boiled
olive oil

Frances says: You're still not sure exactly how it happened, but somehow your neat little handbag that once held a lipstick and boyfriend's keys is now full of Cheerios, crackers, or just crumbs. This is the magic stage, the time when a baby will eat anything, so long as you and everyone within sight is eating it, too. Eating becomes a social activity and tasting what everyone else is eating means being part of the gang.

join the gang

Elisabeth says: The recipes in this section are family dishes from around the world, real classics, the kind of meals you remember when you're far from home. Most, though not all, are based on a grain food sauced with something soupy. Meat is used sparingly: grain food is the mainstay of everyone's daily diet. Most are prepared in a single pot—cooking implements and heat sources were precious when these recipes were first devised.

3

Scotch broth

A lamb stew thick with vegetables and fortified with barley, a Scotch broth is usually served as the main course of a family meal. The barley provides the basic grain food, taking the place of oatcakes or bread.

Serves 2 children and 2 adults

1 pound, 10 ounces neck of lamb, cut into chunks
½ cup barley, soaked for 3–4 hours or overnight
2¼ pounds potatoes, peeled and cut into chunks
2 large carrots, scraped and chopped
2 good-sized leeks, trimmed and sliced
1–2 bay leaves
salt and pepper
a handful of frozen peas (optional)

Put the meat into a roomy heavy pot along with the barley and its soaking water, the potatoes, carrots, leeks, bay leaves, and salt and pepper. Add enough water to submerge everything completely, bring to a boil, reduce the heat, cover, and simmer gently for 1 hour.

Alternatively, cook in a casserole dish in the oven at 350°F. When the meat is soft enough to eat with a spoon and the potatoes have almost collapsed into the broth, it's done. This should take around 25 to 30 minutes, but check every now and again and add more water if it looks like drying out.

For added child appeal, finish the pot with a handful of frozen peas, allowing them just long enough to defrost in the hot broth.

winter minestrone

A cold-beating one-pot dish from northern Italy which takes its name from the meal at which it's traditionally eaten—*minestra*, the midday break. You can vary the composition as you please: a sunny summer minestrone might include chopped tomato instead of carrot and a hank of shredded zucchini blossom to replace the cabbage. If you were preparing this in a Tuscan farmhouse kitchen, you'd drop a slice of garlic-rubbed bread in the bottom of the plate before you ladled in the soup.

Warm the oil in a large soup pot and add the onion, carrots, celery, and chopped prosciutto. Stir everything over the heat for 3–4 minutes to soften the vegetables, but don't let them brown. Add 6 cups water, bring to a boil, reduce the heat, and simmer for 10 minutes. Add the parsley, bay leaf, and potatoes. Simmer for another 10 minutes. Add the pasta and return the pot to a boil. Give it 10 minutes and stir in the shredded greens. Let it bubble up for another 5 minutes, until the vegetables and the pasta are both perfectly tender, the broth has almost all been absorbed, and the soup is thick enough to hold a wooden spoon upright for a second or two.

Taste, and add a little salt—the Tuscans get most of their salt from antipasto, and prefer their bread unsalted. So that people can add their own finishing touches, pass around a cruet of olive oil, thick slices of country bread with a cut garlic clove to rub on the crumb, and a chunk of Parmesan with a grater.

For *pasta e fagioli*—pasta with beans—stir in a cupful of pre-cooked white cannellini beans.

Serves 2 children and 2 adults

2 tablespoons extra virgin olive oil
1 large onion, peeled and diced
2–3 large carrots, scraped and chopped
2–3 celery stalks, rinsed and chopped
1 tablespoon chopped prosciutto
1 tablespoon chopped flat-leaf parsley
1 bay leaf
2 large potatoes, peeled and chopped
2 tablespoons short macaroni or any medium-sized pasta
a handful of dark cabbage leaves (cavalo nero or spring greens), shredded
salt

avocado with tortilla chips and black beans
guacamole con nachos y frijoles

Mexico is where avocados come from and guacamole is the Aztec word for something mashed up. Avocados are a miracle foodstuff: they contain just about everything a person needs to keep body and soul together—particularly when eaten with corn tortillas, the bread of the Aztecs. Avocados are high in protein, rich in fiber and carbohydrates, well endowed with all essential vitamins and minerals, and, better still for babies, they're easily digested. High levels of copper and iron in easily assimilable form make them good for anemia. What more can anyone ask?

Combined with other little things that taste good—shredded chicken, beans, fresh white cheese, a few slivers of fiery green chile—this dish is an adventure in flavors as well as a complete meal in itself.

If your avocados are hard, wrap them in newspaper and store in a warm place for 3–4 days to ripen. Store ripe avocados wrapped in paper in the salad compartment of the fridge: if you keep them in the fridge in a plastic bag, they'll spoil as soon as they meet the air.

Cut the avocados in half, remove the pits, scoop out the flesh, and mash roughly with a fork—don't puree. Fork in the lime or lemon juice, chopped cilantro, and salt. You can add the chile to the mash, or provide it on the side for people to stir in their own to taste.

Cut the tortillas into triangles—known in Mexico as nachos, these are the most convenient for scooping. For a tostada, leave the tortilla whole (makes a great edible plate); for chilaquiles, cut into strips (good for adding to soups); for totopos, cut into squares (good for salting and nibbling). Heat a depth of about 3/4 inch oil in a wide pan and drop in the nachos, a few at a time, wait till they crisp and take a little colour (corn tortillas take longer than wheat-flour), then turn them to gild the other side.

Serve the crisp nachos with the guacamole. On the side for people to choose what they want, offer crumbled white cheese, shredded chicken, and black beans—nicer heated and mashed in a little oil, a preparation known as *frijoles refritos*, refried beans.

Serves 2 children and 2 adults

For the guacamole
2 large, perfectly ripe avocados
juice of 2–3 limes or 1 large lemon
1 tablespoon chopped cilantro
½ teaspoon sea salt
1–2 green chiles, seeded
 and chopped

For the nachos
8 small corn tortillas
 (or 4 large wheat-flour tortillas)
oil for shallow-frying

For the accompaniments
about 1–1½ cups shredded
 cooked chicken
about 1½–2 cups fresh, crumbly
 white cheese (Mexican *queso
 fresco* or Greek feta)
about 3 cups ready-cooked
 black beans

poppy-seed dumplings
pirozhki

Like Italian ravioli, Chinese jiaozi, Mexican tamales, and no doubt a thousand other variations on the same theme, these bite-sized dumplings from Poland, pirozhki (the diminutive of *pirog*, pie) depend upon skill and patience. The dough can be leavened or unleavened and the filling can be anything you please: typical of the Polish kitchen are mushroom cooked with onion, ground pork with buckwheat (kasha), and potato with sauerkraut, as well as the soft white cheese beaten with poppy seeds I have given here. The method of cooking can be frying, baking, steaming, or boiling.

If you have any dough left over, save it for soup noodles: roll it out thinly, cut into little squares or diamonds, and dry on a baking rack in a warm corner of the kitchen.

First make the wrapper dough. Sift the flour and salt into a bowl and make a well in the middle with your fist. Crack in the eggs and add the oil. Mix the wet stuff into the dry—easily done in an electric mixer—and add enough water to make a softish dough. Knead vigorously, massaging it with your knuckles and the flat of your hand, until smooth and no longer sticky. Flour lightly, drop into a plastic bag, and set aside to rest for 30 minutes.

Meanwhile mix the filling ingredients together lightly; don't overbeat and crush the delicate little seeds.

Roll out the dough thinly on a well-floured board, and cut out 2-inch-diameter circles. Put 1 teaspoon of filling in the middle of each circle, wet the edges, and fold them in half, pressing the edges together to enclose the dough. Continue until all the filling is used up.

Bring a large pot of salted water to a boil. Drop in the pirozhki a few at a time. Wait until they bob to the surface, let them simmer for 2 minutes, then drain and transfer to a warm bowl. Toss lightly with melted butter as each batch is dropped into the bowl. Finish with more melted butter and an extra sprinkling of poppy seeds.

Serves 2 children and 2 adults

For the wrapper
9 ounces (2 cups) bread flour
1 teaspoon salt
2 organic cage-free eggs
1 teaspoon oil
about 2 tablespoons cold water

For the filling
1 organic cage-free egg,
beaten lightly with a fork to blend
6 ounces (¾ cup) curd cheese
¼ cup poppy seeds
½ teaspoon freshly grated nutmeg
½ teaspoon salt

For finishing
2–3 tablespoons melted butter
poppy seeds

fresh egg noodles with cheese
spëtzle mit käse

This is one of the simplest and quickest of noodle preparations which, when layered and finished, makes a most superior macaroni and cheese. Once you understand the basics, all the preparation should take no more than 30 minutes from start to finish. It's the highlight of Sunday dinner in the farmhouses of the Black Forest—with a big dish of sliced cold meats and a choice of salads to start, and something substantial in the way of dessert to follow.

In Germany they sell spetzle-makers, instruments that look like large garlic-crushers with uneven holes and produce a similar result to hand scraping. Or you can buy ready-made spetzle in a package: practical and quick, though not as good and not nearly so much fun.

Sift the flour and salt into a bowl. Beat the eggs with a fork until well blended. In a food processor or by hand, work the eggs into the flour until you have a soft, runny dough which still manages to hold its shape; you may need a little water or more flour, depending upon the size of the eggs. Have ready a small wooden scraping-board with a handle—the wrong side of a butter bat or something similar which can be held in the fist—and a small knife. The alternative is a colander and a wooden spoon to push the mixture through the holes.

Preheat the oven to 350°F. Fry the bread crumbs in the butter until golden and set aside. Bring a large pot of salted water to a rolling boil. Heat up a serving bowl, and set a slotted spoon and the cheese close to hand.

If using a board, spread a couple of spoonfuls of the runny egg paste onto the end of it. Using the full length of the knife blade, flick slivers of the egg paste into the boiling water—only enough to cover the surface of the water. Alternatively, press the noodles in small batches through the large holes of the colander held over the boiling water. The spetzle will puff up and firm in a minute or two. As soon as they're done, scoop them up with a slotted spoon, drop them into the serving bowl and sprinkle with a layer of cheese. Continue layering until the spetzle and cheese are all used up. Top with the fried bread crumbs and bake for 10 minutes to set the layers. It's very rich, so serve sparingly, even though a Black Forester could manage the whole thing. A salad of apple and shredded cabbage will cut the richness.

Serves 2 children and 2 adults

About 14 ounces (3 cups)
   bread flour
½ teaspoon salt
4 large organic cage-free eggs
2–3 tablespoons fresh
   bread crumbs
a large pat of butter
10 ounces cheese, grated

macaroni with wild rabbit
maccheroni alla cacciatora

In Italy, pasta—large tubular macaroni shapes of a kind suitable for healthy appetites—is sauced with whatever the hunter brings home. Rabbit, venison, pigeon, partridge, quail, and wild boar are all suitable for this traditional recipe. Wild meat, free-range and additive-free by nature, is lean, dense, of uncertain age, and comes from creatures that have spent their lives romping around the countryside. It needs long, gentle cooking to tenderize it and bring out the flavor, and a little goes a long way.

Put the rabbit, venison, or wild boar meat in a large saucepan with half the chopped onion and carrot (reserve the other half), the celery, optional wine, peppercorns, and a little salt. Add water to cover everything completely. Bring to a boil, reduce the heat to a simmer, cover, and let it bubble gently for 1–1 1/2 hours, until the meat is tender. You may need to add a little more water if the broth looks like drying out. Transfer everything to a strainer set over a bowl to catch the broth, and pick out the bones from the meat, if using rabbit. Return the meat to the broth, discarding the mushy vegetables—they have already done their best—and tip back into the saucepan.

To finish, heat the olive oil in a small frying pan, add the reserved onion and carrot, the garlic and pancetta or bacon, and fry gently until everything takes a little color and softens—about 5 minutes. Stir the contents of the frying pan into the meat and broth in the saucepan. Let it bubble up, reduce the heat, add the olives and parsley, and simmer gently for another 20–30 minutes, to marry the flavors.

Meanwhile, cook the pasta in plenty of lightly salted water, or according to the instructions on the package—15–20 minutes—until it is tender. Drain it, but not too thoroughly, toss with the sauce, and serve in a warm bowl into which you have trickled a little olive oil.

Serves 2 children and 2 adults

1 rabbit, jointed or 1 pound,
10 ounces venison or wild
boar meat, chopped
1 large onion, peeled and chopped
2 large carrots, scraped
and chopped
2 celery stalks
⅔ cup white wine
(optional but nice)
½ teaspoon black peppercorns

For finishing
2–3 tablespoons olive oil
1 garlic clove, skinned and
finely chopped
1 tablespoon chopped pancetta
or lean bacon
1 tablespoon black olives
1 tablespoon chopped parsley

For the pasta
12 ounces large tubular pasta
(mostaccioli, macaroni, rigatoni, ziti)

pasta with pork
fideu a la catalana

The Catalan national dish is a delicately spiced pork and almond noodle paella which is made in much the same way as the Valencian rice paella. Sometimes, though not always, it includes seafood.

Heat the oil in a paella pan or large frying pan until a faint blue haze rises. Add the meat and onion, sprinkle with a little salt, and fry until both ingredients lose their water and begin to caramelize, but don't let them burn. Turn the heat right down, loosely cover, and continue to cook until the meat is firm—a sign that it's cooked right through. Remove the lid and let it bubble up until the pan-juices are oily rather than damp. Push the meat and onions aside and stir in the pasta. Fry until it browns a little. Add the chopped tomatoes and let them bubble up.

Meanwhile, prepare the flavoring paste. Heat the oil in a small frying pan and fry the almonds until golden. Add the garlic and continue to fry for another minute until the garlic softens and picks up color. Add the spices and parsley and toss them over the heat for a minute or two until the scents rise. Add the saffron and its soaking water, let it bubble up, then transfer the contents of the pan to a food processor and whizz to a paste.

Stir the flavoring paste into the pasta, with 1 1/4 cups hot water. Stir again, let it bubble up, reduce the heat, and cook gently until the pasta is tender and the surface is beginning to look dry rather than soupy. Add another splash of boiling water if it looks like drying out. The pasta should be tender and juicy rather than soupy.

Serve with lemon quarters for squeezing and crisp lettuce leaves for scooping.

Serves 2 children and 2 adults

2 tablespoons olive oil
about 1 cup finely
  chopped lean pork
1 medium onion, peeled and
  finely chopped or slivered
salt
9 ounces short pasta
2 ripe tomatoes, skinned
  and chopped

For the flavoring paste
1 tablespoon olive oil
1 tablespoon blanched almonds,
  roughly chopped
2 garlic cloves, skinned and
  chopped
1 teaspoon pimentón
  (Spanish paprika)
1/2 teaspoon ground cinnamon
1/4 teaspoon ground cloves
1 tablespoon chopped parsley
6 saffron strands, soaked in
  1 tablespoon boiling water

For serving
1 lemon, quartered
romaine lettuce

rice noodles with coconut milk and shrimp

laksa lemak

Rice noodles bathed in a spicy coconut broth topped with shrimp is a special Sunday lunch for the Nonya population of Singapore and Malaysia. Nonya are a marriage of migrant Chinese workers and the local women, and the spicings in a laksa reflect the mix.

Rice is the main grain food in Southeast Asia, and noodles made with milled rice are eaten in much the same way as pasta in Italy, as an alternative to bread. The main protein source of the region is seafood, particularly shrimp which thrive in the rice paddies and mangrove swamps, though lots of different insects and reptiles—including snakes, lizards, and ants' eggs—are also eaten.

Soak the rice noodles in a bowl of very hot water for 10 minutes to swell, then drain and toss with 1 tablespoon of the oil. Divide between four serving bowls, top with the bean sprouts, and set aside.

Drop the rest of the oil, the lemongrass, and the shrimp paste, fish sauce or anchovies into a blender, add the onions or shallots, and the turmeric, and grind to a paste. Transfer to a roomy pot and fry gently until the mixture smells fragrant, stirring to prevent burning. Add the coconut milk, let it bubble up, add the shrimp, and let it bubble up again just long enough for the shrimp to turn opaque. Taste and add salt. Ladle the coconut milk and shrimp into the bowls of noodles and finish each portion with a few leaves of cilantro and a mint sprig. Serve with quartered limes for squeezing and chile sliced for those who like it hot—Malay children quickly acquire a high tolerance for chile.

Serves 2 children and 2 adults

9 ounces rice noodles
4 tablespoons oil (sesame or soy)
4 ounces bean sprouts, rinsed and trimmed of any brown bits
1 teaspoon finely chopped lemongrass
2 tablespoons dried shrimp paste or fish sauce or 2 salted anchovies
2 small onions or shallots, peeled and finely chopped
1 teaspoon ground turmeric
2½ cups coconut milk
9 ounces raw shrimp
salt

For serving
a few fresh cilantro leaves
4 small sprigs of fresh mint
1 lime, quartered
fresh green chiles, seeded and sliced, to taste

saffron rice with lentils and dates
addas pillau

This buttery pilau from Iran, layered with lentils sweetened with raisins and dates, is cheap and delicious. The lentils give the rice a pink tinge and the rice is cooked so as to produce a crisp crust. Serve with pitta for scooping, or any of the Middle Eastern flatbreads.

Wash the rice thoroughly in a strainer until the water runs clear. Transfer the rice to a bowl, cover generously with cold water, sprinkle with a little salt, and let it soak for 3–4 hours. Cook the lentils in enough water to cover them to a depth of 2 fingers, allowing 30–40 minutes, until they're perfectly tender and the water has almost all been absorbed. Stir in the dates and raisins, and set aside.

Meanwhile, drain the rice. Bring a large pan of lightly salted water to a boil and stir in the rice. Return the water to a boil, let it bubble up for 3 minutes, then tip the rice into a strainer and rinse under a hot faucet. Remove a ladleful of the rice, put it in a bowl, and stir in the soaked saffron with its water.

Rinse the pan, return it to the heat along with the oil and 2 tablespoons water. Heat until the water evaporates and the oil is clear. Spread in the saffron-tinted rice and fry for a minute or two to evaporate excess water. Top with half the lentils, spread with another layer of rice, top with the rest of the lentils and finish with another layer of rice, mounding it into a dome shape. Poke three holes right through the rice with the handle of a wooden spoon. Wrap the pan lid in a clean dishtowel and cover the pan tightly. Cook the rice on a high heat for 2–3 minutes to reheat it, then turn the heat right down and cook very gently for 30 minutes—longer if you want. Or layer everything into a casserole dish and bake in the oven at 325°F for 30–40 minutes, until the rice is perfectly tender.

Remove the pan from the heat and set the bottom in cold water to loosen the golden crust which you hope has formed underneath. Scoop out the rest of the rice and lentils onto a warm serving plate and trickle with the melted butter. Carefully unstick the crisp crust and drop it onto the buttery mound—if the pan hasn't managed to produce a crust, no matter—better luck next time.

Serves 2 children and 2 adults

1¾ cups long-grain (basmati) rice
sea salt
1⅓ cups green lentils
2 tablespoons chopped fresh dates
1 tablespoon seedless raisins
¼ teaspoon powdered saffron, soaked in 2 tablespoons boiling water
2 tablespoons oil

For serving
2 tablespoons melted unsalted butter

Lentils have a special place in the food mythology of the Middle East as promoters of happiness and bringers of prosperity. In Egypt, they are considered mind-expanding, heart-warming and therefore good for children: brain food with added cheerfulness.

yellow rice with coconut milk
nasi kuning

In Southeast Asia, rice is eaten at every meal in much the same way as bread is in wheat-growing areas. When colored and spiced, rice can provide the centerpiece of a family meal. In this Javanese dish, a mound of golden rice cooked in coconut milk is flavored with cloves, lime leaves, and lemongrass, and finished with ribbons of plain-cooked omelet.

Soak the rice for 1 hour in enough water to cover.

Drain and transfer to a saucepan along with the coconut milk, turmeric, cloves, lime leaves, and lemongrass, and add a little salt. Bring to a boil, reduce the heat, cover, and simmer for 5 minutes, until all the coconut milk has been absorbed.

Turn the heat right down, cover again, and cook very gently for another 10 minutes, until the rice is tender. Remove from the stove, wrap the whole pan in a towel, and leave for at least 20 minutes for the rice to dry and finish swelling.

Meanwhile, beat the eggs together with a pinch of salt until well blended. Heat the oil in an omelet pan and add the eggs, rolling them around the pan so that they form a flat pancake. Remove it as soon as it sets and cut into narrow ribbons.

Remove the lime leaves and lemongrass from the rice. Mound it onto a flat serving dish—easiest if you first spoon the rice into a bowl lined with plastic wrap, then invert the whole thing onto the dish. Top the rice with the omelet ribbons and finish with a few lemon basil leaves.

Add sparkle with a couple of Indonesian sambals, little flavoring mixes in which chili and lime juice are the only certainties. Favorites are sambal tomat (chopped tomato, chile, and shallots dressed with lime juice) and sambal terasi (roasted shrimp paste crumbled with chopped chile, sugar, and lime juice). Shrimp chips are the easiest way to provide crunch.

Serves 2 adults and
2 children

1⅓ cups long-grain rice
   (Thai fragrant, for preference)
2½ cups coconut milk
1 teaspoon ground turmeric
3–4 cloves
1–2 kaffir lime leaves
1 lemongrass stalk, crushed
salt

For finishing
2 large organic cage-free eggs
1 tablespoon oil
lemon basil leaves

Louisiana jambalaya

This is true creole cooking: the name is French and African—*jambon à la "ya,"* an African word for rice—and usually features the Spanish mixture of pork and seafood.

Serves 2 children and 2 adults

4–5 tablespoons oil
1 pound, 10 ounces pork ribs,
cut into bite-sized chunks
salt and pepper
2 celery stalks
1 large onion, peeled and
finely chopped
2 garlic cloves, skinned
and finely chopped
1 green pepper, seeded
and chopped
4 ounces okra, topped and tailed
1 pound tomatoes,
skinned and chopped
¾ cup short-grain rice
1 small sprig each of
thyme and sage
2½ cups chicken stock or water

Heat 2 tablespoons of the oil in a heavy frying pan. Fry the ribs, seasoning them with salt and pepper as they brown, then remove and set aside. Add the remaining oil to the hot juices in the pan and fry the celery, onion, garlic, and green pepper gently until soft—don't let anything burn. Add the okra and fry for a couple of minutes, then add the tomatoes and let it bubble up again.

Return the ribs to the pan, stir in the rice, and add the herbs and stock or water. Let it bubble up, reduce the heat, loosely cover, and simmer for about 20 minutes, until the rice is tender: you may need to add a little more water.

Serve with a bottle of Louisiana hot sauce or Tabasco for people to add their own.

chicken with rice and egg
oyako donburi

A satisfying Japanese dish of plain-cooked rice with chicken and eggs, a combination also known as mother-and-child rice.

First cook the rice. In Japan they sell special rice steamers to make it all easy, but the traditional method works well enough. Wash the rice in several changes of water until the water runs clear. Let it drain in a strainer for 30 minutes. Transfer the drained rice to a heavy saucepan, add the cold water, and bring rapidly to a boil over high heat. Cover tightly, turn the heat right down, and cook without lifting the lid for 15 minutes. Turn the heat up again (leave the lid in place), wait for 20 seconds, then remove the pan from the stove. Let it rest, still covered, for another 10 minutes.

Meanwhile, cut the chicken into small, neat cubes, and set aside. Bring the stock, the soy sauce, and the mirin or sherry, if using, to a boil in a medium-sized saucepan. Add the chicken, return to a boil, and cook for 6–8 minutes, until the chicken is opaque and perfectly firm. Pour in the eggs and add all but a spoonful of the sliced scallions—don't mix. Return the broth to a boil, then turn the heat right down, cover, and let it cook very gently for 3–4 minutes, until the eggs are set but still soft.

Divide the rice between individual bowls and ladle in the broth, including equal amounts of chicken and egg. Finish each serving with a few scraps of the reserved scallion, and cover with a lid before serving. Drink the broth from the bowl, slurping as much as you please. In Japan, anyone over three years old is expected to eat with chopsticks. Keep trying: it's not as hard as it looks.

Serves 2 children and 2 adults

2⅔ cups short-grain rice
3¼ cups cold water
1 pound boned, skinned chicken (breast or leg or both)
2 cups chicken stock
6 tablespoons Japanese soy sauce
2 tablespoons mirin or dry sherry (optional)
6 medium organic cage-free eggs, beaten with a fork to blend
6 scallions, trimmed and finely sliced

chickpea stew with chorizo

cocido con chorizo

A robust Spanish one-pot soup-stew flavored with paprika, garlic, and chorizo, and finished with potato and spinach. Every region—every housewife—likes a different combination of beans, vegetables, and meat; some versions include a portion or two of chicken and fresh pork or beef.

Drain the chickpeas and put them in a large pot with enough cold water to cover generously. Bring to a boil and skim off the gray foam that rises. Meanwhile, singe the garlic cloves by holding them on the tip of a knife in a naked flame until the papery covering blackens and the air is filled with the exquisite scent of roasting garlic.

Drop the garlic and chorizo into the pot and add the pimentón, bay leaves, and tomato paste. Return to a boil, reduce the heat, cover loosely, and cook for 1 1/2–2 hours, until the chickpeas are quite soft. If they're old and hard, they'll take longer. Keep the broth at a rolling boil throughout—don't add salt or let the temperature drop or the chickpeas will never soften. Add *boiling* water as and when necessary.

When the chickpeas are perfectly tender, add the potatoes and let the broth bubble up for another 15 minutes. Taste and add salt. Stir in the shredded greens, bring the pot back to a boil and cook for another 5 minutes or so, until the leaves have wilted and the potatoes are soft. Stir in the olive oil and let it bubble up to thicken the juices a little.

A cocido can be served as a single course, or as two courses without a change of plates: the broth first (fortified with noodles if appetites are keen), then the meat and vegetables.

Serves 2 children and 2 adults

2 cups dried chickpeas, soaked
  overnight in cold water to cover
2–3 garlic cloves, unskinned
4 ounces fresh chorizo sausages
1 tablespoon pimentón
  (Spanish paprika)
1–2 bay leaves
1 tablespoon tomato paste (or
  chopped fresh tomato)

For finishing
1 pound potatoes, peeled
  and chopped
salt
1 pound spinach or Swiss chard,
  rinsed and shredded
2–3 tablespoons olive oil

bread risotto with seafood
açorda de mariscos

A juicy bread risotto—here made with salt-cod, Portugal's national foodstuff—the açorda has affinities with Spain's rural bread soups, ancestors of the modern gazpacho. A family dish, nourishing and fortifying, the recipe makes good use of Portugal's robust country bread. In its simplest form, as a soft breadmeal, an açorda is the first dish Portuguese babies share with their parents.

To prepare your own salt-cod, choose middle-cut and make sure it's not too white (a sign it's been bleached) and that there's no trace of pink down the backbone (a sign of insufficient curing). Brush off any loose salt, rinse thoroughly, and set it to soak in plenty of cold water for 48 hours, changing the water whenever you remember. When the flesh is soft and plump, use your fingers to remove the skin and bones, then flake or tear.

Serves 2 children and 2 adults

12 ounces two-day-old country bread
1 large or 2 medium onions, peeled and finely sliced
½ cup olive oil
5 ounces ready-soaked salt-cod, skinned and boned
2¼ pounds tomatoes
3–4 garlic cloves, skinned and roughly chopped
¼ teaspoon black peppercorns, crushed
½ teaspoon coriander seeds, crushed
½ teaspoon dried oregano
5 ounces raw shrimp or chopped monkfish (angler fish)— or both

For finishing
2 tablespoons torn cilantro leaves

Tear the bread into bite-sized pieces and set it to soak in a bowl of water for 2 hours. Squeeze it dry with your hands.

Meanwhile, fry the onion gently in half the olive oil until soft and golden—30 minutes is not too long. Add the soaked cod torn into small pieces. Stew gently for another 10 minutes.

At the same time, put the tomatoes in a roomy stewpot with the rest of the olive oil, the garlic, peppercorns, coriander seeds, and oregano and bring to a boil. Mash with a wooden spoon and cook down to a thick sauce—the tomatoes will need to lose about half their volume.

When the tomatoes are well reduced, tip into a fine mesh strainer set over a bowl and press through the good juices, discarding what remains in the strainer. Tip the juices back into the pan, and stir in the soaked, squeezed-out bread. Add 3 cups cold water, let it bubble up, reduce the heat, and simmer for another 20 minutes until you have a soft, well-flavored bread risotto, a form in which it's perfectly suitable for babies.

Stir the onion and cod into the bread and cook for another 20 minutes, until the bread is perfectly amalgamated with the broth. Toss to separate the crumbs a little and cook for another moment. Lay the shrimp and/or monkfish on top of the crumbs, wait for a few minutes to allow the flesh to turn opaque in the steam, and finish with plenty of freshly torn cilantro leaves.

bread pudding with cheese and ham
panada alla parmigiana

Italian households traditionally save leftover bread—crusty and chewy when raised with a sourdough starter and baked in a wood-fired oven—for a golden-crusted savory bread pudding enriched with eggs and cheese. A fresh tomato sauce adds sparkle: easy to prepare with fresh tomatoes ripe from the field; out of season, canned or bottled are considered just as good.

This dish is traditionally prepared on a Monday morning with a stock made with the carcass of the Sunday chicken and a flavoring of green celery, onion, bay leaf and a few peppercorns or allspice berries.

Preheat the oven to 350°F.

Mix the bread crumbs with the grated cheese and ham or olives, reserving 1 tablespoon of the cheese for the topping. Beat the eggs with the stock and fold into the bread crumbs. Tip the mixture into an oiled baking dish, sprinkle with the reserved cheese, and trickle a little more oil over the top. Bake for 40–50 minutes, until firm, puffy, brown, and bubbling.

Meanwhile, make the tomato sauce. Scald, skin, and chop the tomatoes (if using canned, just cut them into small pieces). Put them into a little pan with the olive oil, garlic, and tomato paste, stir, let it bubble up, reduce the heat, mash with a wooden spoon, and let it simmer down into a thick, jammy sauce—about 20 minutes.

Cut the panada into squares and serve the tomato sauce separately.

Serves 2 children and 2 adults

4 ounces dried-out sourdough
   bread, crumbled
4 ounces parmesan cheese, grated
1 tablespoon chopped prosciutto
   or pitted black olives
4 organic cage-free eggs
2 cups chicken or vegetable stock
1 tablespoon olive oil

For the tomato sauce
1 pound ripe tomatoes (in winter,
   use canned plum tomatoes)
2 tablespoons olive oil
1 garlic clove, skinned and
   finely chopped
1 tablespoon tomato paste
   (optional)

beef and carrot hotpot
hutspot

This is one of Holland's traditional Sunday lunches—brown beans with bacon is the alternative. Here, meat and carrots are gently cooked in a closed pot in their own juices, with onion for flavor and potatoes for body.

Slice the meat into fine slivers, and set aside.

Heat 1 tablespoon of the drippings or oil in a heavy saucepan and fry the meat and carrots, stirring so all sides feel the heat, until they brown a little. Season with a little salt and pepper, add half the water, turn up the heat, cover, and cook gently without opening the pot. Shake it every now and again to avoid sticking, until the moisture has nearly evaporated and the meat is tender—about 30 minutes—then remove and reserve.

Reheat the pan with the remaining drippings or oil and fry the onions gently for 10–15 minutes, until soft and golden brown. Push the onions aside and add the chopped potatoes to the oily juices. Turn up the heat, wait until the potatoes begin to fry, salt them lightly, and add the remaining water, then reduce the heat, cover, and cook gently until the potatoes are soft—15–20 minutes.

Combine the meat and carrots with the potatoes and onions and reheat everything in the rich meat gravy.

Serves 2 children and 2 adults

1 pound lean stewing beef (skirt, for preference)
2 tablespoons beef drippings or oil
2¼ pounds carrots, scraped and finely sliced
salt and pepper
2 cups water
1 pound onions, peeled and slivered vertically
2¼ pounds potatoes, peeled and chopped small

baked eggplant and lamb
papoutsakia

Serves 2 children and 2 adults

2–3 large firm eggplants, peeled
and halved lengthwise
olive oil for frying
2–3 tablespoons grated cheese
(kefalotiri for authenticity)

For the meat sauce
½ pound ground lean lamb
1 large onion, peeled and
finely chopped
1 tablespoon finely
chopped parsley
1 teaspoon ground cinnamon
1 tablespoon tomato paste
½ cup red wine

For the tomato sauce
2 tablespoons olive oil
2 garlic cloves, skinned and
crushed or finely chopped
2½ cups tomato puree or
plum tomatoes, pureed

For the white sauce
¼ cup butter
2 heaped tablespoons
all-purpose flour
2½ cups whole milk
1 large organic cage-free egg,
whisked with a fork to blend
¼ teaspoon freshly
grated nutmeg
salt and pepper

A sophisticated moussaka flavored with cinnamon and nutmeg, a recipe from the island of Cephalonia. In Cephalonia, as in many of the Greek islands, the Venetians were the occupying power in earlier times, leaving everyone with a taste for the spices the merchants of Venice traded with the East.

Make crisscross cuts in the eggplant flesh, heat the oil in a roomy pan, and gently fry the eggplant halves face down. Cook them until soft (they shrink amazingly) and then transfer to a strainer to drain thoroughly, pressing with a spatula to get rid of excess oil.

Meanwhile, put the ingredients for the meat sauce in a saucepan and let everything bubble gently for 1 hour, until the meat is perfectly tender.

In another pan, simmer the ingredients for the tomato sauce for 30 minutes or so, until thick and rich; it should lose about a third of its volume.

In a third pan, make the white sauce: melt the butter and stir in the flour. As soon as it goes sandy, whisk in the milk gradually and continue whisking over the heat until the sauce thickens. Remove, let it cool to finger temperature, then whisk in the egg. Season with nutmeg, salt, and pepper.

Preheat the oven to 350°F.

Arrange the eggplants in a shallow earthenware baking dish, cut side up. Cover with the meat sauce, top with tomato sauce, and finish with the white sauce. Sprinkle with the grated cheese and bake for about 20 minutes, until brown and bubbling— or 30 minutes if you've prepared it ahead and allowed it to cool.

lamb goulash
paprikas

A slow-simmered stew flavored with onions and paprika, one of the few family dishes that relies heavily on meat. Sour cream is optional in Hungary but essential among Austrians, who picked up the recipe when Hungary was part of their empire.

Purists use pork lard rather than oil for the preliminary frying. In Hungary, these things matter.

Trim the meat and cut it up small.

Heat the lard or oil in a large heavy pot and gently fry the onions and garlic until golden. Push the onions aside and add the meat and turn it in the oniony juices. The whole operation will take 10 minutes and is more like stewing than frying. Add $^1/_4$ cup water, stir in the paprika, and season with salt and pepper. Let it bubble up again, cover the pot tightly, reduce the heat, cover and let it stew very gently for 1 hour. Check regularly that the pot has not boiled dry, adding a little water as necessary. When the meat is perfectly tender, turn up the heat and take the lid off the pot. Watch carefully as the juices cook down, and remove it from the heat just before anything burns: paprika is high in sugar and its natural sweetness can easily turn to bitterness.

Serve with small pasta cooked until tender in plenty of boiling lightly salted water. Pass the sour cream around separately, along with a little dish of hot paprika for people to add as they please.

Serves 2 children and 2 adults

1 pound, 10 ouces boned stewing lamb (shoulder is good)
2 tablespoons lard or oil
1 pound, 10 ounces onions, peeled and finely sliced
2 garlic cloves, skinned and chopped
2 tablespoons mild paprika
salt and pepper

For serving
small pasta shapes (elbow-macaroni, ditalini, or homemade noodles)
sour cream
hot paprika

Frances says: I am always amazed at
how children rebel against food. Why sit at a table when
there're forts to build, stories to tell, electric sockets to explore?
What I can't beat, I join. Which doesn't mean turning beans into funny-
faced caterpillars—I just allow the picky one to make a pattern with what's on
the plate, sprinkle on their own cheese, count out their own almonds, take a bowl of
crackers into the tent to feed the monsters in the corners.

life's a game

Elisabeth says: Forget the smiley faces on the pizza—mealtime is a chance for a
little fantasy. And if you're a strictly no-veg person on normal days and you'll
only eat pumpkin when you're pretending to be Cinderella or Prince
Charming, or if rice doesn't look good to you unless it's cooked in a
paella on the beach, or you'll munch your way
through a pork chop because that's what
firemen do—that's fine.

4

Cinderella's midnight feast
pasta with pumpkin and ricotta

This is what Cinderella's coachman did with the golden coach when it turned back into a pumpkin on the stroke of midnight. Cinderella kindly saved some for the prince.

The prince found the dish so delicious and Cinderella so clever—quite apart from being beautiful and having very small feet—that he asked her to marry him at once. But Cinderella said she'd rather marry the coachman and eat pumpkin pasta every day. Let that be a lesson: if you want to marry Cinderella, learn to cook. The same thing applies if you don't want to marry the coachman—not forgetting he was, after all, a rat.

Serves 4 children

9 ounces peeled, cut-up pumpkin
2 tablespoons butter
12 ounces farfalle (pasta bow ties)
4 teaspoons ricotta

Cook the cut-up pumpkin in $^1/4$ cup water in a tightly covered pan for about 10 minutes—the pumpkin should be soft but not mushy—remove and set aside. Reheat the cooking juices, add the butter, and let it bubble up over a fierce heat until reduced to a spoonful, then remove from the heat and stir in the pumpkin pieces.

At the same time, cook the pasta in plenty of boiling salted water according to the instructions on the package: around 6–8 minutes. Drain—not too thoroughly—and toss with the pumpkin and its buttery juices. Serve the ricotta on the side.

fairy-dust
broccoli with parmesan

Remember what happened when Peter Pan shook Tinkerbell's fairy-dust over Wendy and the boys? They flew to Never-Never Land—and so can you. Broccoli is muscle food, and cheese gives you plenty of energy, so the mixture is just right for chasing pirates or rescuing Indian princesses.

Other vegetables might be carrot sticks, cut-up squash, new potatoes. It works with plain pasta, too.

Serves 4 children
18 ounces broccoli florets
parmesan for grating

Bring a pot of water to a rolling boil (don't salt—the cheese is quite salty enough), and drop in the broccoli. Return the water to a boil, reduce the heat to a simmer, cover to avoid steaming up the kitchen, and cook for 6–8 minutes until the florets are tender but the stalks are still firm enough to hold.

Transfer to a colander and run it under cold water to stop the cooking process and allow the broccoli to remain bright green. Arrange on a plate alongside a shower of freshly grated Parmesan.

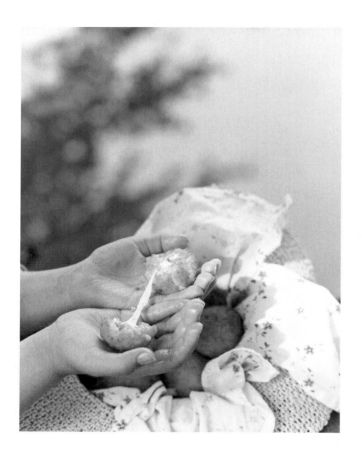

fisherman's piece-for-the-pocket
supplî-al-telefono

Use leftover risotto to make little rice balls, *supplî*, deep-fried in a bread crumb jacket. If you're lucky you'll find a scrap of mozzarella buried in the middle that pulls out into long strings—telephone lines—which makes them *supplî-al-telefono*.

You can, if you like, make the rice balls without any filling at all. Or you can complicate things—add a little sophistication—by including a cube of prosciutto and a dab of tomato sauce or ready-made pesto from a jar.

Mix the rice and egg with your hand, and squidge it thoroughly to make a sticky paste. Spread the bread crumbs on a plate.

Serves 4 children

8 heaped tablespoons leftover risotto
1 large organic cage-free egg, lightly whisked with a fork to blend
about 4 heaped tablespoons dry bread crumbs
12 small cubes mozzarella
olive oil for cooking

Form the rice mixture into a dozen little balls, dampening your hands so it doesn't stick. Push a hole in each ball with your finger and tuck in a cube of mozzarella. Close up the hole neatly and drop each ball into the breadcrumbs, rolling to coat the outside thoroughly. Set aside for the coating to set—10 minutes or overnight.

Preheat the oven to 400°F or heat the oil in a deep-fryer.

To oven-bake, arrange the supplî on a lightly oiled baking tray, brush the tops generously with oil, and bake for 20–25 minutes, until crisp and brown. To deep-fry, slip the supplî, a few at a time, into the hot oil as soon as the surface is lightly hazed with blue; remove when the coating is evenly brown and perfectly crisp and transfer to paper towels to drain.

pirate's breakfast
hot-'n'-sour fishcakes

Spicy Indonesian fishcakes flavored with ginger—what else would a pirate eat for breakfast? You can add a little chili if you like, but don't blame me if the captain makes you walk the plank.

Serves 2 pirates

9 ounces fish fillets, cut into cubes
2 teaspoons ground coriander
1 teaspoon ground cumin
1 teaspoon grated
fresh ginger root
1 tablespoon grated onion
grated zest and juice of ½ lemon
1 egg white, whisked with
a fork to blend
1 tablespoon chopped cilantro
or parsley leaves
¼ cup fresh bread crumbs
salt
2–3 tablespoons oil for frying

Drop the fish cubes into a bowl, checking with your fingers for any little bones. Mix the fish with the spices, grated onion, and lemon zest and juice, cover, and let it marinate for 30 minutes.

Drop the fish and its marinade in a food processor with the egg white, and whizz to a paste. Mix in the chopped cilantro or parsley and the bread crumbs, add a little salt, and form the mixture into 6–8 little patties—easiest if you have a bowl of warm water to dampen your hands.

Heat a little oil in a wok or frying pan.

Slip in the fishcakes a few at a time, and fry, turning them halfway through, until firm and well browned on both sides, allowing about 2 minutes each side. Transfer to paper towels and pat to remove excess oil. Serve with crisp lettuce leaves for wrapping with a handful of rice if you're hungry.

fireman's lunch
grilled pork chops

Every self-respecting New York firefighter goes to work on a chop. Practice your fire drill and eat it on rye with mustard. Caraway improves the digestion, and digestion is important when you're a firefighter in a hurry.

Dust the pork chops on both sides with salt, pepper, and a pinch of caraway. Brush on both sides with a little oil.

Preheat a ridged grill pan. As soon as it is good and hot, sear the chops on both sides —wait until the meat blackens in stripes. Reduce the heat, cover, and cook for 8–10 minutes, turning once, until the juices no longer run pink. Remove and keep warm.

Drop the rye bread on the hot pan and let it pick up the juices from the meat, crisping the crumb where it hits the metal.

Sandwich each chop, bones and all, between 2 slices of rye—you can spread it with butter and mustard, or not—and eat it carefully, saving the bones for last.

Serves 2 young firemen in training

2 pork chops, trimmed
salt and pepper
½ teaspoon caraway seeds
a little oil

For serving
4 slices rye bread, toasted
butter (optional)
mild mustard (optional)

sleepover party
lettuce and bacon soup

Eating lettuce makes you sleepy. Remember when Flopsy, Mopsy, Cottontail, and Peter Rabbit went to sleep in Mr. McGregor's lettuce patch and nearly found themselves popped into Mrs. McGregor's pie?

Shred the lettuce leaves, including the dark outer leaves. Put the chopped potato, bacon, and scallion in a large saucepan with just enough water to cover. You shouldn't need extra salt—the bacon has enough salt already. Bring to a boil, reduce the heat, and simmer for 10–15 minutes, until the potato is perfectly soft. Mash the potato into the cooking broth, add the milk, and bring everything back to a boil. Stir in the shredded lettuce, return to a boil, and cook for another 5 minutes, until the lettuce has collapsed into the soup and turned it a beautiful grass green.

Serves 2 sleepy people

1 lettuce, rinsed
1 medium potato, cut up small
1 tablespoon chopped bacon
1 scallion, finely chopped
2½ cups whole milk

princess-and-the-pea pancakes
apple and cinnamon drop-scones

Everyone knows that princesses are so sensitive they can feel a pea through any number of feather mattresses...which is just as well for the Prince, or how would he know who was the real Princess? Feathery pancakes lightened with apple and flavored with cinnamon are just the thing for a royal tea party. Cinnamon makes things taste sweeter than they really are—useful when you don't want people to overdose on sugar.

Sift the flour into a bowl with the cinnamon, baking powder, and cream of tartar. Whisk the egg with a little of the milk and beat it into the flour mixture with a wooden spoon. Stir in the grated apple and work in enough milk to make a thickish, pourable cream which blankets the back of the spoon. Or drop everything in a blender and blend thoroughly; you may need to add a little more flour if the batter is too thin to hold its shape on the griddle or frying pan.

Set a griddle or heavy frying pan over a medium heat and rub it with a little butter or oil (a clean scrap of linen is useful). When the surface is lightly smoking, drop on a spoonful of batter—the bigger the spoon, the larger the pancake. After a minute, you'll notice bubbles forming on the surface. When the bubbles pop and form little craters, flip the pancake over to cook the other side.

Pile the pancakes in a clean cloth to keep them warm while you finish using the rest of the batter mixture. Tuck just one pea between the layers.

Makes about 12

½ cup all-purpose plain flour
1 teaspoon ground cinnamon
½ teaspoon baking powder
¼ teaspoon cream of tartar
1 egg
about ⅔ cup milk
½ eating apple, rinsed and grated, including the skin
a little butter or oil for greasing
1 pea

beach party paella
saffron rice with chicken and ham

Serves 3–4 children and 2 adults

2–3 tablespoons olive oil
1–2 garlic cloves, skinned and finely chopped
2 ounces serrano ham or chorizo, chopped
½ small free-range chicken, cut into bite-sized pieces
12 ounces short-grain (risotto or pudding) rice
½ teaspoon (about 6) saffron threads, soaked in a little boiling water
salt

Spanish children—and their moms, dads, aunties, uncles, and grandparents—head for the beach on Sunday for a paella party. The proper cooking implement is a *paellera*, a broad, shallow cooking pan with handles at either side which sits on the embers of a campfire. A large frying pan set on the barbecue works just as well.

If you're using a barbecue, light the charcoal about 30 minutes before you're ready to cook. If you're cooking over a camp fire and using a paella pan, wait until the fire burns down to a circle of embers before you set the pan on the heat. If you're cooking at the stove, a frying pan will do.

As soon as the pan is good and hot, add 2 tablespoons olive oil and swirl it around to cover the bottom of the pan.

The best way to eat a paella is to sit around the pan in a circle and eat the portion directly in front of you, using a romaine lettuce leaf as a scoop. You won't need a knife or a plate, though a spoon might come in handy for scraping up the delicious crispy bits at the bottom of the pan.

Fry the garlic and ham or chorizo over a medium heat for 1–2 minutes—long enough for the garlic to soften. Add the chicken pieces and turn them patiently over the heat until cooked right through—you may need to sprinkle them with a little water to keep the heat low. When the juices no longer run pink, add a little more oil and sprinkle in the rice. Stir for a few minutes, until the grains turn opaque.

Add the saffron and its soaking water and enough fresh water to submerge everything completely—roughly 2 parts water to 1 part rice. Add a little salt. Let it bubble up, move the pan further from the heat, and cook gently without stirring for 15 minutes, adding more water as the surface dries out. It's ready when the surface is pitted with tiny craters. Remove from the heat, cover with a thick cloth, and let it sit for 10 minutes for the rice to finish swelling.

treehouse picnic
banana bread with cinnamon and pecans

An undemanding recipe and a good one, a tea-bread that is sticky and gooey enough not to need buttering. No one can climb trees with buttery fingers.

Preheat the oven to 350°F. Butter a 9 × 5-inch loaf pan and line it with buttered baking parchment (banana bread is a bit of a sticker).

Sift the flour with the baking powder and the cinnamon. Peel and cut up the bananas and drop them in a food processor or blender along with the honey and eggs. Whizz to a smooth puree. Meanwhile, beat the butter with the sugar until light and white. Fold the banana mixture into the butter and sugar, alternating with the sifted, spiced flour, and turn thoroughly until there are no pockets of dry flour. Stir in the nuts.

Spoon the cake batter into the prepared pan, spreading it well into the corners. Transfer to the oven and bake for 1 hour, until the cake has shrunk from the sides and is well risen and springy in the middle. Check after 40 minutes and cover the top with foil if it looks like burning.

Wait for 10 minutes for the crumb to loosen from the pan before tipping the loaf out onto a wire rack to cool. It's all the better for a few days in a pan.

Makes a 2-pound loaf

½ cup (1 stick) plus 1 tablespoon
  butter, softened, plus extra
  for greasing
9 ounces self-rising flour
1 teaspoon baking powder
1 teaspoon ground cinnamon
18 ounces very ripe bananas
  (3 large fruits)
4 ounces honey
2 large organic cage-free eggs,
  lightly whisked
½ cup unbleached granulated sugar
½ cup shelled pecans or walnuts,
  roughly broken

Frances says: Sniff 'n' seek is a game invented by Sophie's dad when Sophie wouldn't eat up her breakfast. It takes energy and commitment—so what else is new? First comes sniff, which is what happens when Dad inspects the bowlful; and then seek, which follows when the bowl has been wiped clean and everyone has to hide. Dad finds them by following the scent—and the food has been polished off in the name of fun!

sniff 'n' seek

Elisabeth says: Scent and taste together make flavor. Some things are smellier and tastier than others: garlic, cheese, onion, lemon, and fish are all scents everyone can easily recognize, even if they've never tried them before. The game provides an opportunity for a little gentle persuasion—new and stronger tastes can be introduced precisely because they're less familiar than the bland foods that may be eaten every day.

5

bean soup with basil
soupe au pistou

A bean soup from Provence, very simple and clean-flavored, colored with basil and olive oil. The Provençal pistou is thickened with bread, while Italy's *pisto genovese* has pine nuts.

You can replace the pistou with ready-made pesto if you like, but it won't be as bright and sparky. For a more substantial dish, add a handful each of macaroni and shredded greens. The inhabitants of Nice are particularly fond of Swiss chard, *blea* as it's called in the Provençal language, a fondness that has earned them rather a rude nickname which you couldn't possibly guess—could you?

Scents for sniffing: garlic, basil
Serves 2 children and 2 adults

1¼ cups dried white navy or cranberry beans, soaked overnight
2 green celery stalks, chopped small
1 small onion or shallot, peeled and chopped small
3–4 peppercorns, crushed
2–3 whole cloves
1 large potato, peeled and chopped
salt and pepper

For the pistou
2 garlic cloves, skinned and roughly chopped
4 heaped tablespoons basil leaves
1 thick slice day-old bread
sea salt or kosher salt
⅔ cup olive oil

Drain the beans and rinse them. Put them in a roomy pot with the celery, onion or shallot, peppercorns, cloves, and enough water to cover—no salt. Bring to a rolling boil, skim off any gray foam that bubbles up to the top, reduce the heat, cover, and simmer gently for 1 hour—add more boiling water if needed—until the beans are soft. Stir in the potato and let it bubble up for another 30 minutes, until everything's perfectly tender. Taste, add salt and pepper, and mash the beans a little to thicken the broth.

Make the pistou just before you're ready to serve: drop all the ingredients except the oil into a blender and blend to a puree; keeping the blades moving, add the oil slowly in a steady stream, as if making mayonnaise, until thick and shiny.

Ladle the pale, creamy soup into bowls and serve the bright green sauce separately, so everyone can stir in as much or as little as they please.

cheesy potatoes
aligot

Mashed potatoes all stringy with cheese, just as they like them in the Auvergne—French cheese-making territory—where it's really cold in winter. This dish is traditionally served at weddings in the spring, when the cows are producing plenty of creamy milk and the cheese is young and fresh. The perfect cheese is a young Cantal, still crumbly and sharp; but any other fresh, flaky, white cheese will do.

Boil the potatoes in their skins in enough salted water to cover—start them in cold water. When they're perfectly tender—about 20 minutes after the pot reaches the boil—drain and leave them in the colander until they're just cool enough to handle. Slip off the skins, return the potatoes to the pan, set over a low heat, and mash them thoroughly, beating to remove any lumps.

Meanwhile, in a small pan, bring the milk and the butter gently to a boil along with the garlic. Beat the hot liquid into the mashed potato. Sprinkle in the cheese and beat it in with a wooden spoon, lifting the spoon high to incorporate as much air as possible. As soon as the cheese melts and the mixture is light and fluffy, remove from the heat. Serve in hot bowls and eat with a spoon.

As a variation, make a dent in the middle of each portion and drop in an egg yolk. If you stir it in quickly, it'll cook a little in the heat.

Scents for sniffing:
cheese, garlic
Serves 2 children and 2 adults

2¼ pounds floury potatoes
salt
⅔ cup hot whole milk
½ cup unsalted butter, cut up
2 garlic cloves, skinned and
　crushed
9 ounces young, crumbly,
　white cheese, coarsely grated
4 egg yolks (optional)

mussels with oven fries

moules frites

Freshly cooked mussels eaten straight from the shell with a heap of crisp fries—moules frites, the Belgian national snack—are about as good as it gets. No need to flavor the cooking broth with garlic and parsley: fresh seafood needs no help.

Mussels are a natural crop, even when they're farmed. The spat (tiny mussels) swim around until they find a perch—rocks on the tide-line, posts set close to the shore, ropes hanging from rafts moored in clean water in a bay — and settle down to grow, feeding off whatever floats by. Rope-grown and pole-grown mussels have clean shells with a golden-brown tinge and are flatter and narrower in shape than rock-grown mussels, which have thick, battered, blue-black shells and are usually loaded down with a crop of little barnacles.

Drop the mussels into a bowl of water while you make the fries.

Preheat the oven to 400°F.

Spread the prepared potatoes in an oiled baking tray, brush with more oil, and sprinkle with a little salt. Bake for 30–40 minutes, until the insides are soft and the outsides deliciously crisp and brown.

Meanwhile, scrub the mussels and rinse them well, rejecting any that don't shut when handled, or that are heavy for their size (they're probably full of sand). Use a sharp knife to scrape off the beards—the dark, whiskery tassels that stick out of the shell. Once the mussels have been debearded, you need to cook them within the hour—they won't stay alive for long.

As soon as the fries are out of the oven, cook the mussels. Tip them into a roomy pot with a glass of water and a little salt, bring to a boil, tightly cover, and let them open in the steam, shaking every now and then; 4–5 minutes should do the trick. When the shells have opened, they're done. At this stage, reject any that stay shut. Remove the pan from the heat immediately and serve in bowls. Don't reheat—shellfish toughens if it's overcooked.

Serve the mussels with the fries, warning everyone to be careful not to burn their tongues. A half-shell makes a good scoop.

Scent for sniffing: seafood fresh from the sea
Serves 2 children

18 ounces live mussels

For the oven fries
2 large potatoes, peeled and cut into fat strips
2 tablespoons mild olive oil
sea salt or kosher salt

meatballs with cream sauce

köttbullar

Bite-sized meatballs flavored with nutmeg—a spice from the South Seas with a warm, slightly gingery flavor—are finished in a rose-pink cream sauce in this favorite supper dish from Sweden.

Scent for sniffing: nutmeg
Serves 2 children and
2 adults

18 ounces ground pork or
veal (or half and half)
4 ounces fresh bread crumbs
⅔ cup milk
1 tablespoon finely chopped or
grated onion
1 organic cage-free egg
½ teaspoon freshly grated nutmeg
salt and pepper

For finishing
butter for frying
1 teaspoon flour
⅔ cup sour cream
1 tablespoon tomato paste
(optional)

For serving
new potatoes
cranberries

If you're in a hurry, use ready-made pork bulk sausage—empty the meat from the skins if necessary—flavor it with nutmeg, roll it into little balls, and dust them with flour ready for frying. Just don't tell the Swedes.

Put all the meatball ingredients in a bowl and knead thoroughly until smooth—have a bowl of warm water beside you for rinsing sticky fingers while you work. Or drop everything in a food processor and pound to a paste. Shape the mixture into bite-sized balls—the smaller the children, the smaller the balls.

Melt the butter in a roomy pan over medium heat. As soon as it foams, add the meatballs and cook them gently, turning to brown all sides. Remove as soon as they are completely firm: 6–8 minutes. Sprinkle the flour into the pan, stirring to incorporate the sticky juices, add $1/4$ cup water and bubble up, scraping in all the little brown bits. Stir in the sour cream and the tomato paste, if using, return the meat-balls to the pan and let it all bubble up again. That's all.

Serve with new potatoes (the Swedes grow lovely almond-shaped ones with nutty yellow flesh) and cranberries cooked with a sprinkling of sugar: buy fresh berries, put in a pan with a little water, and simmer until they pop.

chicken rice
with lemongrass
and lime leaves

khao man kai

Chicken and rice are both delicate enough to accept the flavor of other ingredients. This is a Thai dish to eat with a spoon on a cold winter's night. Lime leaves (whole) and lemongrass (sliced or pounded) both freeze well—just pop them into a plastic bag, store in the freezer and shake out as needed.

Rinse the chicken and remove any fat from inside the cavity.

Settle the bird, breast upwards, in a pot and pour in enough cold water to submerge it completely. Bring to a boil, skim off any gray foam that rises, and add the remaining ingredients. Return to a boil, then reduce the heat to a gentle simmer, cover, and poach delicately without letting it boil for about 1 hour, adding more hot water if necessary. If you prefer, transfer the pot to the oven once the poaching water has come to a boil, and let it bubble away quietly at 325°F. The chicken is done when the thigh waggles easily in the socket.

Let it cool in its cooking broth for 30 minutes. Remove the chicken, skin it, and strip all the meat from the bones. Meanwhile, bring 4 cups of the broth to a boil and stir in the rice. Let it bubble up until the rice is soft and the broth has almost all been absorbed, about 20–25 minutes—the dish should be soupy rather than dry. Serve the rice hot with the chicken at room temperature.

Scent for sniffing: lemongrass
Serves 2 children and
2 adults

1 small free-range chicken
1 small onion, peeled and
   quartered
2–3 celery stalks, rinsed and
   chopped
1–2 carrots, scraped and chopped
1 tablespoon chopped lemongrass
   (heart only)
2–3 kaffir lime leaves
1 teaspoon sea salt or kosher salt

For finishing
1⅓ cups Thai fragrant rice

garlic chicken
pollo al ajillo

Scent for sniffing: garlic
Serves 2 children and
2 adults

1 small free-range chicken, cut up
1–2 heaping tablespoons flour
1 tablespoon pimentón (Spanish
paprika)
salt and pepper
4–5 tablespoons olive oil
1 whole garlic head, separated into
cloves, unskinned
2 tablespoons water or white wine

Perfect for sniff'n'seek is this Spanish dish of chicken pieces cooked in olive oil with plenty of garlic. Garlic is very mild and sweet when slow-roasted in its skin. For nibbling, add a choice of little tapas, Spanish-style—useful on a day when you have lots of leftovers in the fridge. Maybe a dish of fried red pepper strips, a handful of baby tomatoes, and a few ears of fresh corn on the cob (drop them in boiling water for a few minutes and they're ready).

Chop the chicken portions into bite-sized pieces and pop them into a plastic bag along with the flour, pimentón, and a little salt and pepper.

Heat the olive oil in a heavy frying pan. Add the chicken pieces and the garlic cloves, and turn everything in the hot oil until the chicken and the garlic brown a little. Turn the heat right down and sprinkle in the water or white wine. Cover loosely and cook gently over a low heat for 20–30 minutes, until the chicken is cooked through and the juices have almost evaporated, leaving a sticky little sauce of garlicky oil.

So that everyone can have a chance to pick and choose, serve the chicken on one dish and the garlic cloves on another.

lamb korma with cardamom
korma chalau

A mild curry from Afghanistan flavored with cardamom and cooked with rice. Afghans take some of their cooking habits from China, some from India and the rest from the Persians.

Cardamom is a small green or black pod about the size of a fingernail filled with oily little seeds. If you heat the seeds gently in a dry pan they smell warm and gingery—which is not surprising as they belong to the ginger family. Some people add them to coffee, or chew them to make their breath smell sweet.

Scents for sniffing: cardamom
Serves 2 children and 2 adults

1 pound, 10 ounces boned
shoulder of lamb
¼ cup plain yogurt
2 tablespoons unsalted butter
or vegetable oil
1 onion, peeled and finely chopped
6 cardamom pods, lightly crushed
1 teaspoon crushed or powdered
saffron
1⅓ cups short-grain rice
salt

Cut the lamb into bite-sized cubes. Put it in a bowl, mix in the yogurt, and let it marinate for an hour or so to tenderize the meat.

Heat the clarified butter or oil in a heavy pan and fry the onion gently for 10 minutes, until soft and golden. Add the cardamom seeds—once the pods are crushed, the seeds can easily be separated from them—and fry for another minute, until the mixture smells gingery. Stir in the saffron and add the lamb and its yogurty juices. Let it bubble up, reduce the heat, loosely cover, and simmer for 40–60 minutes, until the meat is tender.

Meanwhile, rinse the rice in a strainer until the water runs clear. Put it in a bowl with enough water to cover and let it soak for 30 minutes, then drain.

Add 2 1/2 cups water to the lamb in the pan and reheat until boiling. Stir in the rice, let it bubble up again, salt lightly, reduce the heat and cook gently for 20–30 minutes, until the rice grains are soft and the juices have almost all been absorbed.

Pork braised with cinnamon and onions
hirino stifado

The Greeks like to use cinnamon in a stifado, a winter stew with onions, because the flavor is warm and a little sweet, reminding them of summer sunshine.

Trim the meat, discarding any gristle but leaving the fat—it'll melt during the cooking, tenderizing the meat.

Heat the oil in a roomy heavy pan and fry the shallots or onions gently, shaking the pan over the heat until they brown a little. Push them to one side or remove and reserve. Add the meat, carrot, and celery, and fry until the meat takes a little color. Add the raisins, cinnamon, orange peel, bay leaf, and enough water to cover everything completely, returning the whole onions to the pan if you've taken them out.

Season with a little salt and pepper; let it bubble up, reduce the heat, and simmer gently, loosely covered, for an hour or so, until the meat is perfectly tender and the juices are cooked right down. Add the potato and a mug of boiling water, bring it back to a boil, reduce the heat again, cover and simmer for another 12–15 minutes, until the potatoes are tender and their starch has thickened the juices a little. Taste and check the seasoning; if it's a little sweet, sharpen it up with 1 tablespoon red wine vinegar.

Remove the cinnamon stick if you can find it and serve the stifado warm—no Greek likes food piping hot.

As a variation, instead of the potatoes, try including chunks of quince—they have a delicate flowery flavor and a slightly gritty texture rather like a pear.

Scents for sniffing: cinnamon, orange peel, bay
Serves 2 children and 2 adults

18 ounces boned pork, chopped
2–3 tablespoons olive oil
18 ounces baby shallots or pickling onions, peeled
1 large carrot, scraped and chopped
2 celery stalks, rinsed and chopped
1 tablespoon raisins
1 short piece cinnamon stick
a curl of orange peel (dried is best)
1 bay leaf
salt and pepper

For finishing
18 ounces potatoes, peeled and cut into bite-sized pieces
1 tablespoon red wine vinegar (optional)

all-pork sausages
bratwurst

German sausages are made with well-ground pork and no rusk or bread crumbs at all, unlike most sausages—which is why it's worth making your own. You can form the mixture into patties: there's no need to hunt around for sausage casings, which, these days, are both hard to find and rarely natural.

In Germany, the proper accompaniment is fresh horseradish grated into long, thin strings and mild German mustard which has a delicate, spicy flavor.

Work the meat thoroughly with the seasonings—use your hands and have beside you a bowl of warm water for rinsing. Form the mixture into fat sausage shapes or round patties and dust them with a little flour.

Heat a heavy frying pan or grill pan. Fry or grill the sausages or patties—you may need a little oil—until perfectly firm and nicely browned. Check that the juices no longer run pink before you take them off the heat.

Good with plain boiled potatoes and a mushy apple sauce.

Scents for sniffing: allspice, marjoram
Serves 2 children and 2 adults

18 ounces finely ground pork shoulder
1 teaspoon ground allspice
1 teaspoon crumbled dried marjoram
½ teaspoon salt
¼ teaspoon ground white pepper
flour for dusting

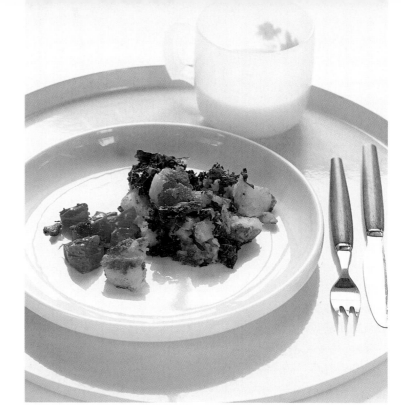

old clothes
roupa velha

Greens and potatoes cooked to a crisp crust with salty scraps of wind-dried ham (in Portugal *presunto*) produce a raggedy dish known as *roupa velha*, old clothes. Recipes for potatoes fried with greens pop up under different names—bubble and squeak, hash, scouse—wherever potatoes are grown and people need something cheap and tasty for supper.

Scraps of salt-cod (*bacalhau*, Portugal's favorite ingredient) can replace the meat, or you might like to pop a fried egg on top. Portuguese children like this dish with a few drops of piri-piri, a ferocious chili sauce from Brazil.

Cook the potatoes in plenty of boiling water until soft—about 20 minutes. Dump the greens on top of the potatoes after they've been on the boil for 15 minutes. Drain both vegetables as soon as the potatoes are soft and the greens are tender but still bright.

If you're using a pan that doesn't have a non-stick surface, heat it first before you add the oil—preliminary heating ensures nothing sticks to the metal. Fry the chopped ham or bacon in the oil for 1 minute, then add the garlic and cook for 2 minutes—don't let it brown. Add the potatoes and greens and let them fry gently, stirring and turning over the mixture as it browns and crisps. When you have a beautifully crusty heap of greens and potato, push it aside to make a space for the tomatoes. Add the tomatoes and fry for another 2 minutes, to soften and brown the tomato skins a little. No need to add salt—there's plenty in the ham.

Scent for sniffing: greens
Serves 2 children and
2 adults

4 large potatoes, peeled
  and cut into chunks
2 large handfuls of shredded
  greens: savoy or sweetheart
  cabbage, brussels sprouts, turnip
  greens
about 2 tablespoons olive oil
2 tablespoons chopped *presunto*
  (Portuguese prosciutto) or
  lean bacon
2 garlic cloves, skinned and slivered
12 baby tomatoes, cut in half
  or quartered

Frances says: Something strange happens. You call in the babysitter, a friend or granny, and when you come home you are amazed to hear what the kids will eat when Mom and Dad are not around. You are also told that they have been as good as gold and were asleep as soon as their heads went down—and in their own beds. What's going on? Simple. Someone else did the cooking or sent out for take-out food. If they think it came in a carton, they'll eat it.

the take-out trick

Elisabeth says: Every parent has a favorite exotic take-out dish, something that tasted good at a certain time and that for ever afterwards is a reminder of people and places and fun. For a child, the attraction is the unfamiliar, the element which is not everyday but excitingly somewhere else—like a sunshine holiday in the middle of winter, or climbing on a plane for the first time, and knowing you're going to a place you've never visited before.

6

ramadan lentil soup
harira

The Ramadan take-out dish is a spicy soup eaten immediately after sunset during the month-long fast which devout Muslims observe by eating only during the hours of darkness. When the muezzin calls at nightfall, working people hurry to the nearest marketplace for their plateful of soup—everyone's too hungry to wait. And anyway, the aroma of spices is irresistible. This version comes from Lebanon. The recipe is very variable: some like chickpeas or fava beans instead of lentils, others use different spicings—every region, every town or village has its preference.

In a roomy soup pot, fry the shallots or scallions and garlic gently in the oil until soft and golden—don't let them brown. Add the lentils and stir over the heat. Pour in 8 cups of water and add the spices and a little salt. Bring to a boil, reduce the heat, and simmer for 10 minutes.

Add the chopped potato, return to a boil, and cook gently for another 30 minutes, until the lentils are soupy and the potato perfectly soft. Taste and adjust the seasoning.

Finish with a sprinkle of cilantro leaves and finely chopped scallions, with the chile on the side for people to add what they please.

Serves 2 children and 2 adults

2 shallots or 4–5 scallions, finely chopped
2–3 garlic cloves, skinned and finely chopped
3–4 tablespoons oil
2¾ cups dried green lentils
I short piece cinnamon stick
I teaspoon cumin seeds
½ teaspoon cracked black pepper
I large potato, peeled and chopped
salt and pepper

For finishing
small bunch of cilantro
2–3 scallions, finely chopped
finely chopped green chile

Japanese noodles with tahini dressing

The cheapest of New York's take-out dishes, noodles with sesame dressing are a nutritious food fix appreciated by busy mothers and time-pressed office workers alike. The noodles in this recipe are Japanese —either *soba* (the thin, brown, buckwheat variety) or *udon* (thick, brown and made of wheat flour); the tahini dressing is, well, basically Middle Eastern, though sesame— *goma*—is very much part of Japanese cuisine, both as an oil and as a seed.

Bring a large pot of water to a boil (no salt). Add the noodles and stir to separate the strands. Return the water to a boil and cook uncovered for 5 minutes, stirring regularly. Transfer to a colander, reserving 2 tablespoons of the cooking water. Rinse the noodles through with cold water to stop the cooking process, tip into a bowl, and toss with a tablespoon of the sesame oil.

Meanwhile, toast the sesame seeds in the remaining sesame oil in a small pan for 1–2 minutes, stirring until the seeds brown—take care they don't burn.

Bring the reserved cooking water back to a boil and mix it with the soy sauce and the tahini. Toss the noodles in this sauce and finish with the toasted sesame seeds.

Serves 2 children and 2 adults

9 ounces *soba* or *udon* noodles
2 tablespoons sesame oil
1 heaping tablespoon
   sesame seeds
2 tablespoons soy sauce
2 tablespoons tahini
   (sesame paste)

Singapore fried noodles

su chow mein

A noodle-based stir-fry with a pinch of curry seasoning, just as they like it in Singapore where the Indian influence is strong. It's quick, too: once all the ingredients are prepared, it'll take no more than 5 minutes from the moment the heat hits the pan.

Chow mein is a leftover dish into which anything goes (within reason), so the recipes are very variable. Chinese egg noodles, Italian vermicelli, or thin spaghetti are all a suitable pasta base. Bean sprouts, blanched broccoli florets, or slivered water chestnuts can replace the carrot, and the scallions can be substituted by leek cut into matchsticks or by slivered garlic. The curry powder can be omitted or replaced with freshly milled pepper or chopped chile if, like Singapore's children, you like a little heat in your food.

Serves 2 children and 2 adults

9 ounces cellophane (bean-thread)
or rice noodles
2–3 tablespoons light oil
(soy or sunflower)
2 organic cage-free eggs
1 large carrot, scraped and
cut into matchsticks
2–3 scallions, trimmed and cut
into diamonds
2–3 tablespoons shredded leftover
roast pork or chopped bacon or
cooked, peeled shrimp
1 teaspoon curry powder
about 1 tablespoon light soy sauce

Soak the noodles in boiling water in a bowl for 20 minutes or so, or according to the instructions on the package. Fork them over every now and again to loosen the threads. Drain and toss with a little oil to stop them sticking together.

Meanwhile, prepare the rest of the ingredients. Whisk the eggs with a fork to blend and then heat 1 tablespoon of the oil in a wok or roomy frying pan. Pour in the egg mixture and let it set in a thin pancake. Take it out, roll it up, and cut into narrow ribbons; set aside.

Add the remaining oil to the pan and toss in the carrot and scallions. Add the pork, bacon, or shrimp and turn the vegetables in the hot oil until the carrot softens a little. Sprinkle in the curry powder and stir-fry to blend and develop the flavors. Toss in the noodles and the egg ribbons, turning them to blend thoroughly and allow the noodles to heat, and sprinkle in the soy sauce.

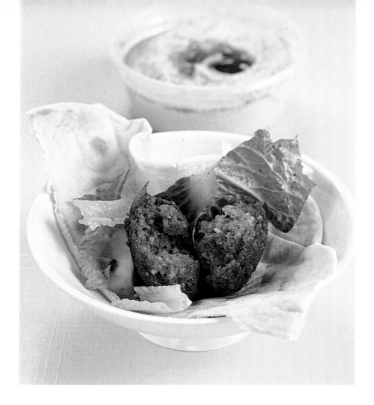

chickpea fritters with sesame sauce

falafel bin tahini

These crisp little fritters are everyone's favorite street food throughout the Middle East—you'll find them in Egypt, the Lebanon, Israel, and all points between. Cooked to order and stuffed into a hot pita-bread pocket with a fistful of salad and a dollop of garlicky hummus, together they make a meal.

You can buy a packaged falafel mix in stores which stock Middle Eastern foods. The Egyptians make theirs with fava beans, the Israelis with chickpeas. In the Lebanon, they like white beans. Each to his own.

Serves 2 children and 2 adults

9 ounces chickpeas, soaked overnight
1 teaspoon ground cumin
½ teaspoon salt
½ teaspoon baking powder
1 tablespoon finely chopped onion
1 tablespoon finely chopped parsley
1 tablespoon finely chopped cilantro
oil for frying

For the tahini dip
9 ounces tahini (sesame seed paste)
juice of 1 lemon
1 garlic clove, skinned and finely chopped
½ teaspoon salt

Drain the chickpeas and dry them very thoroughly in a clean cloth. Drop them into a food processor and blend to a very smooth paste: they must be very dry and very well crushed or the fritters will fall apart as soon as they hit the hot oil. Add the rest of the ingredients (apart from the oil) in the order given, blending between each addition, until you have a thick paste. Set it aside for 1 hour or so to let it rest and firm up.

Meanwhile, make the tahini dip: mix all the ingredients together until well blended, then taste to see if you need a little more salt or lemon juice.

When you're ready to fry, break off walnut-sized pieces of the chickpea paste, work each into a small ball, and arrange on a lightly oiled plate or place between two sheets of plastic wrap. Flatten the balls with the back of a spoon to form little patties.

Heat a deep-fryer or, if using a frying pan, heat enough oil to submerge the patties completely. Wait until a faint blue haze rises and test the temperature with a cube of bread—bubbles should form immediately around the edge and it should brown within 10 seconds. Push the patties, a few at a time, from the plate into the hot oil with a spatula—don't try to pick them up in your fingers. If the oil is too hot, the patties will splutter and split; if it's too cool, the patties will fall to pieces. Should this happen, remove any debris, adjust the temperature, and start again.

Fry the patties until the outer shell crisps and browns—the inside will cook in the steam. Transfer the first batch to paper towels with a slotted spoon, keep warm, and continue until the mixture is all used up.

Serve with pita bread and hefty lettuce leaves (add cucumber sticks, sliced tomato, and onion if you like), with the tahini dip on the side. Eat the falafel as hot as you can bear—they're no good cold.

greens with peanuts
msamba

This is a popular fast food in the street markets of South Africa, where it's made with a variety of edible leaves, including collard greens and the leaves of pumpkin, squash, sweet potato, and yam. African cooks like to present clean flavors in simple combinations.

Cook the spinach in a tightly covered pot in the water that clings to the leaves after washing—sprinkle with salt to encourage the juices to run. As soon as the leaves collapse and soften, remove the lid and add a layer of chopped tomatoes and scallions. Sprinkle with the powdered peanuts, but do not stir. Reduce the heat, cover loosely, and simmer for about 15 minutes, until the tomato flesh has softened in the steam. Stir, cover loosely again, and simmer for another 15 minutes. Remove the lid and let it bubble up fiercely to concentrate the juices.

Serve with a ladleful of *putu-pap*, the cornmeal porridge of the region. Soft polenta is also a good substitute. Msamba is also good with grilled corn on the cob—don't add salt, just a squeeze of lime juice to balance the natural sweetness.

Serves 2 children and 2 adults

1 pound, 10 ounces spinach or
  other greens
½ teaspoon salt
18 ounces tomatoes, finely
  chopped
6–8 scallions, finely chopped
¼ cup roasted peanuts,
  finely powdered in a food
  processor

Dominican kidney beans and rice
habichuelas con arroz

A soupy dish of rice cooked with red beans colored and flavored with *sazón*, a tomato and red-pepper seasoning-mix fried in a little oil. Cheap and nutritious, rice-and-beans (a variable dish throughout the Caribbean) is sold by the ladleful in every Hispanic take-out place in New York.

Drain the beans and transfer them to a pan with 3 times their own volume of cold water. Bring them to a boil without salt. Keep them gently bubbling until soft—about 1½ hours. To cook in a pressure cooker, allow 30 minutes.

Put the rice to soak in cold water while you prepare the *sazón*. Heat the oil in a pan and gently fry the garlic, onion, and red pepper to soften—allow 10 minutes, and don't let them brown. Add the tomato, let it bubble up, and cook for another 5 minutes, mashing with a wooden spoon, until soft and mushy.

Stir the drained beans into the sauce, add their own volume of boiling water, and let it bubble up. Drain the rice and stir it into the beans. Add about 2 cups boiling water, enough to soften the rice and make a little sauce. Cover, and simmer gently until most of the liquid has been absorbed and the rice is tender; you may need a little more boiling water. The result should be soupy, spoonable, and prettily tinged with pink. Offer salt and pepper so that people can season their own.

Wash it down with a chilled bottle of Sorrel Pop, a refreshing infusion of hibiscus flowers and cinnamon available in any West Indian grocery store.

Serves 2 children and 2 adults

9 ounces dried pinto or cranberry or red kidney beans, soaked overnight
1⅓ cups long-grain rice

For the sazón
2 tablespoons oil
2 garlic cloves, skinned and finely chopped
1 medium onion, peeled and finely chopped
½ red pepper, seeded and finely chopped
1 large tomato, skinned and finely chopped (or 1 tablespoon tomato paste)

The choice of beans varies from island to island: alternatives include black-eyed peas, cow-peas, gingko beans, chickpeas, black beans, navy, or haricot beans.

rice-paper wrapper rolls
nem

You'll find a Vietnamese *nem* stand in a corner of every French market, a legacy of France's colonial involvement in Southeast Asia. The rice-paper crêpes used as wrappers, *galettes de riz*, are ready-cooked. They can be soaked, rolled around a filling, and fried—usual in French markets—or simply soaked and used as a soft wrapper for raw vegetables.

To rehydrate the crêpes from the package, fill a shallow dish or roasting pan with boiling water and submerge each crêpe one by one for 15 seconds, just long enough to soften and swell. Transfer carefully to a damp cloth and cover with another damp cloth, ready for stuffing.

Pick over the bean sprouts and tweak off any little brown tails. Mix the bean sprouts, the vegetable matchsticks, and shredded chicken with the egg whisked up with the soy sauce. Place a line of filling on one side of each wrapper and roll it up until you reach the middle. Flip over the sides to enclose the filling, and continue to roll until you have a neat little cigar shape. Repeat until the vegetable mixture is all used up (if you have extra filling, just soak another wrapper).

Heat a wok or frying pan, and pour in enough oil just to submerge the rolls. As soon as a faint blue haze rises, slip in the *nem*, only 3 or 4 at a time or the oil will cool and the wrappers won't crisp. As soon as they bubble and gild—don't let them brown—roll them over to finish the other side. Transfer to paper towels to drain.

Serve with lettuce leaves and mint leaves for wrapping, and a little dipping sauce of rice-wine vinegar flavored with ginger.

Variation: To serve *nem* uncooked, as summer rolls—nice when the weather's hot and steamy—arrange the prepared vegetables and the pre-soaked crêpes ready for rolling, and set everything out on the table. Each person takes a crêpe and fills it with vegetables, shredded chicken, shredded lettuce and mint leaves, sprinkled with soy sauce, then rolls it up into a little package, tucking in one end and leaving the other end open. Eat it from the open end.

Serves 2 children and 2 adults

8–12 *nem* wrappers
(rice-paper wrappers, *banh trang*)
4 ounces bean sprouts
2 leeks or 4 scallions, trimmed, and
cut into matchsticks
2 carrots, scraped and cut
into matchsticks
2 tablespoons shredded chicken
1 teaspoon fresh ginger root, cut
into matchsticks
1 organic cage-free egg
1 tablespoon soy sauce

For finishing
oil for deep-frying
lettuce and mint leaves
for wrapping
rice-wine vinegar and ginger
for dipping

cheese phyllo-pastry pie
pita sa kajmak

A popular take-out dish in Belgrade's central market in Serbia, where it's sold by weight, warm from the oven. Call it the quiche of the eastern Mediterranean: the filling is fresh, clean, and a perfect match for the crisp, delicate crust. This is the basic recipe—as with the French quiche, you can add other things to the filling: chopped bacon or ham, mushrooms sautéed in butter, chopped cooked spinach.

Preheat the oven to 350°F. Melt the butter in a small pan, skim any foam off the top, and pour the clear golden liquid off, leaving the milk solids behind. Reserve.

Cut the phyllo sheets in half to give you 8 sheets, each 7 x 9 inch, and separate, taking care to keep the pastry dough covered while you work; it dries out and cracks very easily. Using a pastry brush dipped in the melted butter, butter a small pie pan, diameter about 6 inches. Line it with 2 sheets of the phyllo dough, leaving the edges flopping loose—they'll be tucked up and over the filling later. Dip the brush back in the butter and sprinkle some over the phyllo in the pan. Lay on another 2 sheets, and sprinkle with butter, making 4 thicknesses in all.

Fork up the eggs in a bowl and beat in the two cheeses. Taste, and add salt if needed—feta's already pretty salty.

Spread the cheese filling lightly over the pastry dough—don't press the air out of the layers. Cover with 2 sheets of phyllo, sprinkle with melted butter, and continue with another couple of layers, leaving the edges loose. Sprinkle with the remaining butter and fold the loose ends delicately up and over the pie, leaving them rumpled and airy like an unmade bed. Sprinkle with a little water from your fingertips.

Bake for 40–50 minutes, until the pastry is crisp and lightly browned and the filling is set. The pie will stay crisp even when cool. Cut into squares or wedges, as you please.

Serves 2 children and 2 adults

½ cup (1 stick) unsalted butter
4 sheets phyllo dough (standard size 14 x 18 inches)
2 large organic cage-free eggs
8-ounce package cream cheese (the real stuff—not low-fat)
4 ounces feta or any other strong cheese, crumbled
salt

Norwegian fish patties

fiskekaker

Little bite-sized fish patties, cooked in butter and made with nothing but ground fish and cream, are sold as a take-out dish from the *fiskemattbutik*, a special ground-fish shop which also sells the same mixture raw—fast food for all the family.

Frozen fish won't do here: it's too watery. Norwegians have instant access to fresh fish—nowhere is more than a few miles from the nearest fjord. In ports such as Bergen, schoolchildren, drawn by the delicious scent of hot butter, line up at lunchtime and take a bagful of *fiskekaker* down to the quayside, swinging their legs over the sea wall and looking out over the ocean as they eat.

Chop the fish flesh roughly, put it in a food processor with the rest of the ingredients, and whizz rapidly to a puree—don't let it overheat or the mixture will separate. Leave for 20 minutes or so in the fridge to firm up.

Heat a heavy frying pan or grill pan. When it's good and hot, drop in a little pat of butter. When it stops sizzling, drop on tablespoons of the fish mixture, patting each spoonful flat with the back of a spoon, and fry, turning once. Don't overcook—allow a maximum of 5 minutes' cooking time for each one. No need to flour the patties—they won't stick.

Serves 2 children and 2 adults

18 ounces filleted white fish (haddock
   is best, cod will do), skinned
6 tablespoons very cold cream
1 tablespoon mashed potato
   or cornstarch
½ teaspoon freshly grated nutmeg
½ teaspoon sea salt or kosher salt
butter for frying

Indonesian satay

The satay-seller peddles his wares up and down the streets of Southeast Asian cities, advertising his presence by the delicious aroma of roasting spices. On special occasions, you can send for your favorite satay man to set up his little portable box-barbecue in the yard and prepare satay for the whole household.

Anyone with a peanut allergy can replace the peanut butter with mashed chickpeas, or omit it altogether and use 2 teaspoons cornstarch for a little extra thickening.

Serves 2 children and 2 adults

18 ounces boneless chicken breast
oil for brushing

For the marinade
1 medium onion, peeled and chopped
2 teaspoons chopped fresh ginger root
2 tablespoons lemon juice
1 tablespoon palm sugar or honey
2 tablespoons sesame oil
2 tablespoons soy sauce

For the sauce
⅔ cup thick coconut milk
¼ cup coarse peanut butter
1 teaspoon cornstarch

Skin the chicken breast and cut into neat cubes. Drop the marinade ingredients into a blender and blend it until smooth. Pour it over the chicken, turn to coat, then cover and let it marinate in the fridge for an hour or so. Meanwhile, set 12 bamboo skewers (satay sticks) to soak in water.

Take the marinated chicken out of the fridge ahead of time for it to return to room temperature. Remove the chicken cubes from the marinade (reserve the juices) and thread them onto the skewers, leaving at least a thumb's width of space at either end.

Make the satay sauce. Scrape the leftover marinade into the blender, add the coconut milk, peanut butter, and cornstarch (blend it first in a spoonful of water) and blend thoroughly. Tip into a small saucepan, bring to a boil, and stir over the heat until the cornstarch cooks and thickens the sauce a little. Remove from the heat and allow to cool to room temperature.

Light the barbecue or preheat the broiler. Set the satay sticks as close as possible to the heat source and turn them regularly so that the heat reaches all sides. Brush with a little oil throughout. Allow 5–6 minutes, until the meat is firm and lightly blackened at the edges. Serve with the satay sauce.

fried chicken with onions
yassa

The secret of this aromatic Senegalese slow-simmered stew is the deliciously thick bed of onions which provides the cooking juices. You'll find it in fast-food outlets in New York's Harlem, where it's ladled over a steaming mound of rice or couscous.

Yassa is what you make of it, a variable dish in which the only certainty is plenty of onion. The chicken can be replaced with meat or fish (for fish, cut the cooking time in half). Or, for a more substantial dish, include yam dumplings or *foo-foo*— pounded cassava meal. For extra greens, stir in shredded cassava leaves or spinach.

Put the chicken pieces in a bowl with the onions, lime juice, salt, and pepper, and turn with your hands to mix everything thoroughly. Cover with plastic wrap and set in a cool place for 3–4 hours—or overnight in the fridge—for the meat to take the flavors.

Remove the chicken pieces and pat dry. Reserve the onions and the marinade.

Heat the oil in a large, heavy, flameproof pan or Dutch oven and fry the chicken pieces in batches until they brown—5–6 minutes, turning regularly. Remove and set aside. Use a slotted spoon to take the onions out of the marinade and stir them into the hot oil in the pan. Add the carrot, celery, and garlic, and fry everything gently until soft and lightly browned—10 minutes or so. Add the reserved marinade and a cup of water and let it bubble up.

Place the chicken on the bed of aromatic vegetables, tightly cover, and cook gently either over a low heat or in the oven at 325°F for 40–50 minutes, until the chicken is perfectly cooked and tender.

Serve ladled over rice or couscous, and hand the chile around separately for people to add their own.

Serves 2 children and 2 adults

2¼ pounds chicken pieces
4 large onions, peeled and
    thinly sliced
⅔ cup lime juice
½ teaspoon salt
¼ teaspoon freshly ground pepper
¼ cup olive oil
1 large carrot, scraped and chopped
1 celery stalk, rinsed and chopped
4 garlic cloves, skinned and
    finely chopped

For serving
steamed rice or couscous
fresh red chile (Scotch bonnet is
    good), seeded and chopped

Frances says: Kids usually get their first taste of unfamiliar cultures when their parents take them to local restaurants. In big cities everywhere, when both parents go out to work all week, most of us don't have time to do everything. Chances are we'll head out on a Saturday evening— at least for a treat—timing ourselves to get there before the rush, to be sure of a warm reception.

the restaurant table

Elisabeth says: What you don't always learn in a restaurant are the table manners —the behavior that fits the food, the pattern of eating you'd expect to find when people of that nationality eat at home. Table manners tell you *how* as well as *what* to eat, something that is not always obvious in restaurants, however authentic the cooking.

So let's pretend...

7

...to eat as they do in France

herb omelet
omelette fines herbes

Serves 1–2

1 large or 2 small organic
cage-free eggs
1 tablespoon chopped fresh herbs
(see below)
a pat of unsalted butter about the
size of a hazelnut
sea salt and pepper

French cooks love fresh herbs
and use lots of them in cooking
and as remedies for minor
illnesses. Only the soft-leaf herbs
are included in omelets—parsley,
chervil, chives, and tarragon are
the most important (thyme,
rosemary, sage, and bay are not
suitable). Tarragon is a bit
anise-like and peppery, chervil
tastes of licorice, chives are
oniony, and parsley tastes carroty
and a little sweet.

One large or two small eggs are just enough to make a juicy, soft-centered, child-sized omelet—grown-ups have two or even three eggs. In a French bistro you can always ask for an omelet, even when it's not on the menu, and you can usually choose the flavoring: fresh herbs are particularly delicious, but there is also cheese, ham, mushroom, tomato—or you can just eat it plain. In France, you'd have it with a green salad of curly, bitter-flavored greens—frisée or curly chicory—dressed with a little oil and wine vinegar.

Lightly blend the egg(s) with a fork and add a small pinch of salt and a very little freshly ground pepper—don't whisk or overmix. Sprinkle in the herbs.

Set a plate to warm beside the stove. Heat a small omelet pan over medium heat and add the butter. When it foams, but before it turns brown, tip in the egg mixture. Holding the handle with one hand and a fork or spatula with the other, move the egg as it cooks, drawing the set egg from the bottom of the pan to form soft, creamy curds. After about 30 seconds, when the curds are just formed but still frothy, stop moving the mixture to allow the bottom to set. Flip one third of the omelet over onto the middle third, wait for 10 seconds, then roll the omelet out onto a warm plate.

For small children, share the omelet between two. It cuts into strips quite easily and is good with sautéed potatoes and a green salad—no tomato or cucumber, just green leaves—dressed with a little olive oil, a drop of wine vinegar, and a pinch of sea salt.

table manners

French children join their parents at the table as soon as they're able to perch on someone's knee. At traditional family meals, three courses are usual and children follow the same eating pattern as the adults. First comes the hors d'oeuvre, something to nibble while the preparation of the main course is finished: a slice of pâté, slivers of wind-dried ham or *saucisson sec* (French salami) with unsalted butter, sliced tomatoes dressed with oil and garlic, carrots with sesame seeds, shredded celeriac (celery root) in a mustardy mayonnaise. The *entrée* or main course is eaten with the same utensils (often on the same plate) and might be meat, fish, poultry, or eggs.

The cheese course follows, served with a green salad. Then comes fruit—fresh in summer, a compote in winter—maybe with *coeur-à-la-crème* (sour cream dripped through a heart-shaped cheese mold), or a spoonful of *fromage frais*, trickled with honey.

Bread is always on the table for mopping plates, particularly between courses. From a very early age, children are offered a drop of red wine in their water to aid digestion.

...to eat as they do in China

rice-paper-wrapped chicken with steamed broccoli

tse bao gai

Little packages of chicken with fresh ginger and scallion taste good, lose none of the nutritional value in the juices, look pretty, and are fun for children to unwrap. On the side, broccoli for balance, shrimp chips for crunch, and plain white rice for bulk. The idea is that dishes that are set on the table at the same time must complement each other and together provide a well-balanced meal.

Put the rice into a roomy saucepan and fill with enough cold water to cover to a depth of 2 fingers. Bring quickly to a boil, turn the heat right down, tightly cover, and steam gently for about 20 minutes, shaking the pan every now and again so that the grains are evenly cooked. Or use a rice steamer.

Meanwhile, prepare the chicken breasts. Slice them across the grain into very thin, bite-sized slivers. Mix the soy sauce with the sesame oil and sugar in a small bowl, add the chicken, ginger, and scallions, turn to coat, and let it marinate for 30 minutes or so. Cut the rice-paper wrappers or parchment into 12 squares about the length of your hand.

When you're ready to cook, preheat the oven to 450°F and set a baking sheet in it to heat. The chicken wraps must be at room temperature before they go in the oven. While the oven is heating, divide the marinated chicken with its ginger and scallions into 12 little oblong piles. Lay out the first square ready to receive its filling. Place one pile of chicken diagonally across one corner, leaving a flap at one end. Fold

Serves 2 children and 2 adults

1 cup long-grain white rice
3 chicken breasts, skinned and boned
2 tablespoons soy sauce
2 tablespoons sesame oil
1 teaspoon sugar
1 tablespoon fresh ginger root, cut into fine matchsticks
4 scallions, trimmed and sliced
1 package rice-paper wrappers or 2–3 sheets baking parchment
18 ounces broccoli, cut into bite-sized florets
1 tablespoon oil and 2 tablespoons oyster sauce (optional)
24 shrimp chips (*kru puk*)

table manners

Chinese children join their parents at the table as babes in arms and are expected to wield their own chopsticks from the age of three. Food is always served in small enough pieces to allow it to be eaten without a knife. All the dishes are set in the middle of the table at the same time, each person has their own bowl of rice and helps themselves from the serving dishes with their own chopsticks, taking only as much as can be eaten in a single mouthful. The division of sweet and savory is not clearly defined, even when the dishes arrive in a succession of courses, as at a banquet.

Combinations matter: for a meal to satisfy the eater's spiritual as well as physical requirements, the *yin* and *yang*—the feminine and masculine elements of all things— must be kept in harmony. Even everyday meals are carefully composed to provide the correct balance of *fan* (grain food) and *cai* (meats and vegetables). Color, shape, aroma, flavor, and texture are also taken into consideration.

In company, it's polite to serve your guests with the best morsels so they don't need to appear greedy by serving themselves.

the flap over the filling and continue to fold until you reach the middle of the wrapper. Fold the two side corners into the middle, enclosing the filling on three sides. Continue folding until you reach the far corner, tucking the flap under to make a firm little envelope. Repeat until you have 12 wraps. Arrange them on the hot baking sheet, brush the tops with oil, and put in the oven for 4–6 minutes, until the meat feels firm when you prod the packet. Let cool a little before serving.

Meanwhile, cook the broccoli in a steamer; alternatively toss it in a wok in a little heated oil, adding enough water to cook it in its own steam, and finish with oyster sauce.

Provide each person with their own bowl of rice and serve the broccoli and chicken wraps separately. If you are using rice-paper wrappers, you can eat the whole wrap; with baking parchment, it will need to be unwrapped—almost as much fun. Freshly cooked shrimp chips—just drop them in hot oil and wait until they puff—provide the crunch. You can also put them in the microwave at 100 per cent for 60 seconds, but they won't taste as good.

...to eat as they do in India

chapatis with potato and spinach curry
alu sag kari

Freshly cooked flatbreads—chapatis, rotis, parathas—are the heart of India's family meals, the most important item on the table, serving as wrapper, pusher, and mopper for other foods. Rice and dhal provide the bulk—cheap, nourishing and easily increased if more guests arrive at the table. Supporting dishes such as this delicately spiced vegetarian curry are chosen for balance, an important consideration when planning an Indian meal. Combinations—soft with crisp, hot with cool, fortifying with refreshing—are carefully considered.

Preparing a chapati dough is easy with a food processor—the reward is really fresh breads hot from the griddle. Sift the flour with $1/2$ teaspoon salt into the processor's bowl and, using the dough hook, gradually add enough warm water to make a soft dough—about 2 cups. Stop as soon it forms a single lump (1–2 minutes). Tip the dough ball out onto a floured board and finish kneading by hand, working it with your fists until it's silky and smooth. Form into a ball, cover with plastic wrap or a damp cloth, and set aside for 1–2 hours for the flour to swell (overnight is best of all).

To prepare the curry, heat the butter or oil in a medium-sized saucepan. Add the onion and fry gently until soft and golden—allow at least 10 minutes. Sprinkle with the garam masala and turmeric, add the potatoes, stir, and add a little salt. Pour in enough water to submerge everything completely. Let it bubble up, then reduce the heat to a gentle simmer, loosely cover, and cook for 20–25 minutes, until the potatoes are perfectly soft and have absorbed most of the golden liquid. Stir in the shredded spinach, turning everything over the heat until the leaves wilt—3–4 minutes.

Just before the family comes to the table, prepare the chapatis for the griddle. Knead the dough ball until smooth—for a minute or two—and roll it into a thick rope.

Serves 2 children and 2 adults

For the chapatis
about 12 ounces chapati flour (*atta*), or 9 ounces stoneground whole-wheat and 4 ounces white bread flour
salt

For the curry
2 tablespoons melted butter or oil
1 large onion, peeled and finely chopped
1 tablespoon garam masala
1 teaspoon ground tumeric
2¼ pounds potatoes, peeled and chopped
11 ounces spinach, shredded
1 tablespoon cashews or almonds, toasted

For the side dishes
plain-cooked dhal
plain-cooked rice (basmati or any long-grain rice)
plain yogurt, stirred with grated cucumber

Break off a nugget about the size of a walnut, keeping the rest covered under plastic wrap, work into a smooth ball, dust lightly with flour, and set it aside under another sheet of plastic wrap. Repeat with the rest of the rope. Flatten and roll each ball into a thin pancake (about 8-inch diameter) between 2 sheets of plastic wrap or waxed paper. Dust lightly on both sides with flour and pile into a bowl, then cover to keep the air out.

Place a heavy iron frying pan or griddle over medium heat. When it's good and hot, wipe the surface with a clean rag dipped in melted butter or oil and drop the first chapati onto it. Wait for 1 minute until little brown blisters appear on the underside. (If the chapati blisters black immediately, the griddle is too hot; if no blisters appear at all, it's too cool.) Turn it and bake the other side for another minute, pressing the edges with a potholder to trap the air in the middle and create bubbles. Continue until all are done, piling the cooked chapatis into a clean cloth.

Meanwhile, reheat the curry and finish it by adding the toasted nuts. Set it on the table along with the side dishes, judging amounts according to appetites. Serve the chapatis in a basket, well wrapped to keep them warm and soft. If you cook on gas, the chapatis can be puffed first: hold each one in the gas flame for a few seconds, then turn it to toast the other side, when, magically, it'll puff up like a balloon.

Each person scoops up a little of whatever they fancy with a torn, bite-sized piece of chapati, taking care to eat neatly and not spoil the dish for others.

table manners

Family ties are strong in India. In traditionally organized households, several generations live under one roof and the day's cooking is shared. Side dishes—curries, dhals, rice—are prepared ahead of time by the senior women working together in the company of children; a small baby is always in someone's arms, dozing between feeds. At the end of the working day and after school, everyone gathers at home for the main meal. Children are taught to eat daintily, with the first two fingers and thumb of the right hand only, picking up small pieces of food with a torn-off corner of a scooping-bread, taking great care not to touch another person's portion. Hindu households are traditionally vegetarian: fish is acceptable, but poultry and meat are eaten sparingly—or not at all if the household is strict Brahmin or Jain. Small bowls of the prepared dishes are laid out on the table ahead of time and replenished when empty, while one person stays in the kitchen to roll and cook the flatbreads. Strict Hindus have to throw away any leftovers, so they are careful not to put too much on the table and never take more than they can eat in one mouthful.

...to eat as they do in Scandinavia

Swedish cold table
smorgasbord

Serves 2 children and 2 adults

**For the brined salmon
(no-fuss gravadlax)**
18 ounces salmon fillet
(tail-piece is fine)
2 tablespoons sea salt or kosher salt
1 tablespoon oil
1 tablespoon chopped fresh dill

**For the herring and
cucumber salad**
9 ounces pickled herrings, chopped
into bite-sized pieces
9 ounces chopped cucumber
½ cup sour cream
1 tablespoon chopped fresh chives

For serving
small new potatoes
fresh dill for flavoring (the
flowerhead, if possible)

A *smorgasbord* without pickled herrings is unthinkable—never mind if you don't like herring, just eat up your gravadlax and thank heaven for new potatoes. The Scandinavian cold table—*smorgasbord*, though only in Sweden—is an arrangement of small dishes, mostly fishy, which can easily be prepared from what's in the pantry, a relaxed way of eating that suits the long summer days when the midnight sun shines and no one ever seems to sleep at all.

Prepare the salmon 2 days ahead. Put the fish, skin-side down, in a china or heatproof glass gratin dish into which it fits snugly. Dissolve the salt in 2½ cups boiling water, let it cool, and pour it over the fish; you need to submerge it completely. Cover the dish with plastic wrap and place in the salad compartment of the refrigerator for 2 days.

Drain and dry the fish. Rub it lightly with the oil and sprinkle with the dill, cover again, and refrigerate until you're ready to eat.

Cook the potatoes with the dill in plenty of lightly salted water—about 15–20 minutes depending upon size. Drain well.

Meanwhile, combine the herrings with the cucumber, sour cream, and chives. Slice the salmon finely into thin wedges, angling the knife across the grain.

Serve everything separately, with crispbread and unsalted butter, followed by a dish of fresh berries to eat with sour cream as a dessert.

table manners

In Scandinavia and throughout northern Europe, children take their main meal of the day with their parents and use plate, fork, and spoon from an early age. In regions where food was traditionally scarce, people took to using plates and table implements early and with enthusiasm, perhaps as a way of imposing order by limiting how much each person ate. In the old days, when rural households might be isolated for long periods by deep snow, the pantry had to be filled during the summer to carry the family through the winter, making everyone aware not only of the season, but also of the need to conserve food in times of plenty against the lean months. The traditional spread provided at gatherings still often includes an element of bring-your-own—each family bringing a dish for sharing—reflecting a very real need, since no one household could afford to empty its pantry all at once.

Appetites were also limited by deciding which foods were to be consumed first, of which the cheapest and most plentiful was herring. To this day, pickled herring dishes are always eaten before anything else.

...to eat as they do in Morocco

Friday couscous with chickpea stew
couscous bin tagine

**Serves 2 children and
2 adults**
(although Middle Easterners
would consider it rude to
count the participants)

9 ounces instant couscous
2–3 tablespoons olive oil
9 ounces baby onions, peeled
1 medium eggplant, chopped
1 large carrot, scraped
and chopped
1 teaspoon cumin seeds
1 teaspoon powdered saffron
1 short piece cinnamon stick
18 ounces tomatoes, skinned and
chopped (canned are fine)
1 tablespoon sliced pitted
green olives
2 tablespoons raisins
9 ounces cooked chickpeas
(canned are fine)

For serving (optional)
1 tablespoon harissa (Moroccan
chili paste)

A fragrant heap of little grains served with an aromatic stew cooked in a tagine (the traditional round-bellied earthenware cooking pot), the Friday couscous is Morocco's equivalent of the Sunday roast.

Heat the oil in a well-tempered earthenware tagine or heavy, large pan. Add the onions, eggplant, and carrot and stir over the heat until the vegetables brown a little on all sides. Sprinkle with the spices, fry for another moment or two, then add the tomatoes. Let it bubble up and add the olives, raisins, and chickpeas. Pour in enough water to submerge everything, let it bubble up again, reduce the heat, loosely cover, and simmer for 20–30 minutes, until the raisins are plump and the cooking juices are well flavored and reduced by half.

Meanwhile, set the instant couscous to soak in boiling water according to the instructions on the package. No need to feel bad about it—instant couscous is as popular with Moroccan housewives as it is elsewhere.

Serve everyone with a helping of couscous and hand the tagine around separately, along with a little bowl of hot sauce made by diluting the harissa paste with a ladleful of the cooking juices.

table manners

Moroccans traditionally eat their food neatly without knife, fork, or spoon, using the first two fingers and thumb of the right hand only, which means that hands must be well washed and everything that is set on the table must be soft enough to break apart one-handed. At a traditionally served meal, each person dips into the same serving dish and eats only from the portion in front of them. To pile your food onto your own plate is considered greedy and bad-mannered—unless, of course, you're a foreigner and cannot be expected to know better.

Moroccan children learn from their mothers to roll the couscous into neat little balls by squidging the grains one-handed in the palm. Mothers with toddlers pop the little balls into their children's open mouths, as if they were feeding baby birds. Sweet things are eaten at other times than the conclusion of a meal: Morocco has a vast repertoire of almond and honey pastries, taken mid-morning or mid-afternoon with a glass of iced water, mint tea, or sherbet (chilled water sweetened with syrup).

...to eat as they do in Japan

miso soup with bean curd
tofu no suimono

Little cubes of creamy bean curd are dropped into a delicate crystal-clear broth, with no further cooking or additions necessary—well, maybe a few slivers of scallion or a sprig of watercress. Miso soup is one of the unsung glories of the Japanese kitchen cupboard: you can buy it as a mix, much like a bouillon cube, or ready-diluted in a carton like orange juice. Bean curd (tofu) can be bought fresh from Oriental grocers or health food stores—rinse, cover with fresh water changed daily, and store in the fridge for no longer than a week. Both miso and tofu are highly nutritious and the combination provides a healthy food fix at any time of day for children as well as grown-ups. It's vegetarian, too.

Heat the miso soup until boiling and ladle it over the cubed tofu in individual bowls. Finish each bowlful with a few scraps of scallion or sprigs of watercress—or not, as you please. That's all.

For nibbling, provide a handful of edamame beans, fresh young soy beans left in the pod and boiled until tender: they're available ready-prepared in Oriental markets, where you'll find them fresh in the summer and frozen at other times of year (it's pretty hard to tell the difference).

Serves 2 children and 2 adults

4 cups low-salt miso soup prepared according to the instructions on the package (or see method)
about 12 ounces fresh bean curd (tofu), drained and cubed
1–2 scallions, sliced diagonally or a few sprigs of watercress (optional)

For nibbling (optional)
ready-cooked edamame beans (fresh soybeans)

table manners

Japanese children take their places on the mat with the adults—chairs and table as an eating arrangement are relatively rare—and are expected to treat their food with respect. The Japanese meal is a formal affair, even at home. The main meal is taken between 6 and 7 p.m. and, for the family, usually features three dishes, each cooked by a different method. On important occasions, more dishes are served, though the number is always uneven: party time can feature five, seven, nine. Servings are small and everyone gets their own little portion of individual dishes, served in carefully chosen bowls and eaten with particularly pointy chopsticks.

At its simplest, a meal consists of rice, relish, and a bowl of clear soup. Eating can be a bit noisy: slurping and belching tell everyone how much you're enjoying what you're eating. It's bad manners to talk of important things while eating—best not to talk at all and concentrate on the presentation, a form of storytelling. Dishes are composed to follow a theme mirroring the seasons. In spring, a carrot might be carved in the shape of a blossom; in autumn, a leaf.

Frances says: From a young age, kids want to be included. Stationary babies imprisoned in the highchair love to shake spice jars like rattles; teething babies suck frozen bagels, cold comfort for sore gums. Toddlers bang pots and pans like a set of drums. And once they discover the science of it all, suddenly, faster than you can imagine, they're cracking eggs, measuring cups of flour, and peering through the oven door to check the progress of something they've cooked.

cooking together

Elisabeth says: Cooking is and should be enjoyable—there's a sense of achievement in seeing the task through from beginning to end. Start with gathering the various cooking implements ready for use and work through the recipe step by step to the moment when the food is set on the table and tasted. Some of these recipes need no cooking, others require the use of the stove. Unplug the telephone, set the cell phone on silent, and have fun.

8

crispbread with soured milk and raspberries

flatbrød med saeterømme og rødbaer

Serves 2 children

1 tablespoon sour cream
or crème fraîche
1¼ cups milk
¼ cup fresh or frozen raspberries
1 tablespoon sugar
1 extra-thin rye crispbread

You need 2 cereal bowls, a spoon, and a small mixing bowl (or, if you are in a hurry, a small saucepan, in which case you also need the stove).

Have you ever wondered how anyone came up with the idea of eating cornflakes with milk for breakfast? Well, it seems that the Norwegians thought of it first. In Norway, where they like to drink soured milk for breakfast, the flakes are made with *flatbrød*—paper-thin crispbreads as big as a bicycle wheel. Combine these with fresh berries in summer and a berry compote in winter. In northern Norway you don't need a freezer to keep your berries frozen in winter—you just store them on the porch.

Stir the sour cream or crème fraîche into the milk, divide it between 2 cereal bowls, cover with plastic wrap, and set in a warm place for 2–3 hours—or a cool place overnight (not the fridge, it's too cold)—until the milk thickens a little. To sour fresh milk without sour cream, squeeze in a little lemon juice: you'll still have to wait until it thickens.

Meanwhile, make the raspberry compote. Stir the raspberries with the sugar in a bowl and let them make juice for the time it takes to set the milk. If you want to hurry them along, put the raspberries and sugar in a saucepan and heat until the juice bubbles and thickens a little—2–3 minutes is all it needs.

When you're ready to eat, crumble the crispbread with your fingers over the soured milk—the flakes should sit on top of the milk until you break the surface with a spoon—and finish with a spoonful of raspberry compote.

Dr. Bircher's Swiss muesli

Makes about 5 cups

9 ounces rolled oats (porridge)
4 ounces dried apricots,
chopped small
⅓ cup raisins or dried cranberries
⅓ cup golden raisins
⅓ cup unskinned almonds, chopped
⅓ cup unskinned hazelnuts, chopped
2 ounces wheat germ
1 tablespoon unrefined brown
sugar (optional)

You need a mixing bowl
and a storage jar. There's no
need for the stove.

Dr. Bircher-Benner, a Swiss physician working at a Zurich clinic in the 1920s, invented the famous mixture as a health cure for his patients. It still tastes good and it does you good, and there's no need to buy it packaged. You can choose other nuts and fruits, but keep the mixture varied for nutritional reasons: every little thing contributes something different.

Mix together all the dry ingredients—the muesli-base—and store in an airtight jar until needed.

To eat, soak in apple juice or milk and wait for 20 minutes until the oats swell—or eat it right away, as you please. Nice with fresh berries or grated apple.

French hazelnut nutella

Makes about 2½ cups

⅔ cup unbleached cane sugar
2½ ounces high-quality
unsweetened cocoa powder
⅔ cup light cream
4 ounces ground hazelnuts

You need a small heavy
saucepan, a wooden spoon,
and 2 sterilized jam jars.
This recipe uses the oven.

I know, I know—no one needs encouragement to eat chocolate and nuts, though nutritionists agree that a peanut butter and jelly sandwich is just about the perfect fuel-food. This is a rough-and-ready version of the chocolate-hazelnut spread adored by French children. For added sophistication, use vanilla-flavored sugar—just bury a whole vanilla bean in the sugar jar and leave it for a week.

Mix the sugar and cocoa in a small heavy saucepan. Stir in the cream and bring the mixture gently to a boil over medium heat, stirring constantly. Reduce the heat and cook for 2 minutes, until the sugar crystals have completely dissolved. Remove from the heat, wait until it cools to finger heat, and stir in the ground hazelnuts, beating until smooth. Pack it into sterilized jam jars and keep it in the fridge for no longer than a week.

Eat the nutella with sourdough bread and raspberry jam—who needs peanut butter and jelly?

Parisian pain au chocolat

The French started it, and now everyone knows what they think this is: a chocolate-stuffed croissant from the bakery, something you'd never dream of making at home. But the real thing is a lot simpler and much more delicious.

What's required is a robust, chewy, just-baked baguette (no fluffy stuff from the supermarket) and the best dark chocolate—grown-up chocolate, not too sweet, with an edge of bitterness.

Push a hole lengthwize through the middle of the baguette with the handle of a wooden spoon. Shove the chocolate into the hole, making sure it's distributed down the full length. That's all.

Serves 1

½ freshly baked baguette
2 ounces very good dark chocolate, at least 70% cocoa solids, broken up

You need a wooden spoon.

New Orleans granola

This is the American version of Dr. Bircher's magic mix (see opposite). It's sweeter and stickier and lumpier and altogether a great deal more delicious, even if it doesn't stick to the ribs in quite the same way.

Preheat the oven to 325°F.

Melt the butter with the honey and sugar in a small saucepan set over a low heat, stirring until the sugar crystals have dissolved completely.

Mix all the dry ingredients in a roomy bowl. Stir in the butter-honey mixture, tossing to blend, though not too thoroughly, letting it form sticky little lumps.

Spread the mixture in a roasting pan. Transfer to the oven and bake, stirring occasionally to prevent sticking, for about 25 minutes, until golden—don't wait until it browns: it'll crisp as it cools. The cooking time depends upon how dry the ingredients were when you began.

Let cool completely before storing in an airtight tin. Eat it by the handful when you're hungry, or settle down with a bowlful topped with milk or cream or yogurt and fresh berries.

Makes about 4–4½ cups

2 tablespoons unsalted butter
3 tablespoons honey
2 tablespoons unrefined brown sugar
9 ounces rolled oats (porridge)
3 tablespoons shelled unsalted sunflower seeds
3 tablespoons grated fresh or desiccated coconut
3 tablespoons shelled unsalted pumpkin seeds
2 tablespoons pine nuts
2 tablespoons shelled pistachios
4 tablespoons slivered almonds

You need a small saucepan, a wooden spoon, a mixing bowl, and a roasting pan. This recipe uses the oven.

Ligurian focaccia
sage and onion pizza-bread

The focaccia is the traditional pizza of northern Italy and is eaten as a snack in much the same way as the southern pizza (an invention, it's believed, of the bakers of Naples). The difference is that focaccia is puffier, thicker, and the toppings are simpler: olive oil and sea salt are the basics. Ligurians particularly like sage and onion, with tomato and rosemary as the alternative.

1 pound, 10 ounces strong white
bread flour (Italians use 00—
double-zero)
1 teaspoon salt
1 ounce rapid-rise yeast
(follow the instructions on the
package) or 2 ounces fresh
(compressed) yeast
½ cup extra virgin olive oil
1 tablespoon sage leaves,
torn in pieces
semolina for dusting

For finishing
olive oil
coarse sea salt
½ red onion, sliced into half moons
1 tablespoon small black olives

You need a large mixing bowl,
a 1-quart glass measuring cup, a
pastry board or clean counter, and
2 baking sheets with lips.
This recipe uses the oven.

Sift the flour into a warm bowl and mix in the salt and yeast (if you're using fresh yeast, rub it into the flour with your fingertips). Mix the oil with about 15 fluid ounces warm water in a glass measuring cup. Make a well in the center of the flour and pour in the water/oil mixture.

Using your hand as a hook, work the oily water into the flour gradually till it all sticks together in a soft, sticky lump. Tip the lump onto a pastry board or clean counter dusted with a little flour, and work it well with your fists till you have a smooth very soft dough ball. Drop it back in the bowl, cover with plastic wrap, and set in a warm place for about an hour, till the dough is light, spongy, and has doubled in size.

Tip the dough back onto the pastry board or counter and punch and pull it till it's completely collapsed—it'll still feel light and spongy—then work in the torn sage. Cut the dough ball in half and form each half into a ball. Rub the palms of your hands with a little oil and pat each dough ball out till you have a fat, round flattened focaccia.

Oil the baking sheets and dust them lightly with semolina. Drop a focaccia on the middle of each sheet and pat it out to cover the whole surface, pushing it into the corners—it should be about as thick as your thumb. Dust the top lightly with more semolina, cover loosely with plastic wrap, and let it rise again for 30 minutes. Meanwhile, preheat the oven to maximum—450°F.

Using the five fingers of one hand, punch the surface of the dough 3 or 4 times to make a pattern of little dimples. Trickle a little oil into the dimples, scatter the top of the dough with coarse salt, and sprinkle with warm water from your fingertips. Scatter with the slivers of onion and the olives.

Transfer the baking sheets to the oven and bake for 20–25 minutes until the bread is puffed and golden. As soon as you take the bread out of the oven, trickle it with a little more oil. Cut into squares and eat your focaccia as hot as you can bear.

Neapolitan calzone

A basic bread dough can't go wrong, once you understand the principles. If you have a gang of boys to keep out of trouble, calzone—slipper-breads, pizzas that have been flipped over to enclose the filling—fit the bill.

Sift the flour into a large bowl and put the bowl into a low-temperature oven for the flour to warm.

Warm a coffee mug by filling it with hot water. Tip out the water and put in the yeast and sugar. Cream the two together (marvelous how the yeast blends with the sugar). Fill up the mug with warm (not hot) water.

Make a well in the middle of the warm flour. Measure in the oil and sprinkle in the salt. Pour in the yeast mixture. Stir it around and add enough warm water to make a soft dough—about 1 1/4 cups. Knead thoroughly, working it well with your fists (very therapeutic). When the dough is smooth and no longer sticky, put the empty mixing bowl back into the low oven to warm it up again. Remove, settle the dough-ball in the warm bowl, and put the whole thing into a plastic bag. Tie the bag loosely and let the dough rise for 40–60 minutes, until puffy and doubled in size.

Preheat the oven to 450°F.

Knead the dough to distribute the air—it'll lose most of its volume—then quarter it, and cut each quarter in 2, giving you 8 pieces of dough. Knead each piece into a ball and flatten it into a thin disc on a floured board (or countertop) with a rolling pin, or else sandwich it between 2 sheets of plastic wrap and press it flat your hands.

Drop a teaspoon of diced ham and cheese in the middle of each disk, wet the edge with a damp finger, and fold one side over the other to enclose the filling. Press the edges together. Continue until all the dough is used up and you have 8 little slipper-shaped pockets.

Arrange the calzones on a lightly oiled baking sheet, transfer to the oven, and bake for 15–20 minutes, until puffed and golden. If you have a deep-fryer (standard equipment in Italian kitchens), you can fry them like doughnuts.

Makes 8 fist-sized calzones

1 pound white bread flour
1 ounce fresh (compressed) yeast
   or ½ ounce dried yeast (follow
   the directions on the package)
½ teaspoon sugar
2 tablespoons olive oil
½ teaspoon salt

For the filling
2 tablespoons chopped
   cooked ham
2 tablespoons cubed mozzarella
   cheese

You need a large mixing bowl and sifter, a mug and spoon, a plastic bag, wooden board (or counter) and rolling pin (or 2 sheets of plastic wrap), and a baking sheet. This recipe uses the oven.

Serves 2 children and
2 adults

For the pasta
10½ ounces pasta flour
(00—double-zero)
½ teaspoon salt
3 organic cage-free eggs
a little olive oil
semolina for dusting

For finishing
a pat of butter
toasted hazelnuts, crushed
honey
yogurt

You need a large and a small
mixing bowl, a fork, plastic wrap, a
rolling pin, a saucepan, a slotted
spoon, a serving bowl, and a frying
pan. This recipe uses the stove.

rags-and-tatters
cenci

This is pasta in its easiest form: a simple, nutritious dough made by kneading flour with egg—nothing added, nothing taken away. And there's no need to mess about with cutting and shaping the pasta: raggedy bits taste interesting and look delicious *because* they're uneven. Children in pasta-making regions such as northern Italy and eastern Europe have it as a treat with nuts, honey, and cream—though you can, of course, finish your pasta any way you like.

Sift the flour with the salt into a roomy bowl and use your fist to make a dip in the middle. Crack the eggs into a small bowl, mix them together with a fork, and then drop them into the dip in the flour. Using your hands, work the eggs into the flour, adding just enough water to make a soft dough; if you save half an eggshell as a measure, you'll need no more than a shellful (1 tablespoon). Keep pushing and pulling the dough until it's smooth and silky. Form it into a ball and rub it with a little oil. Pop the oily ball into a plastic bag and let it rest for 20 minutes.

Dust a board or countertop with semolina. Drop the dough onto the board and divide it into 4 pieces. Work each piece into a ball, flatten it with your palm, and place it between 2 sheets of plastic wrap. Using a rolling pin, roll out each ball as thinly as you can. Remove the plastic wrap and cut the dough into small raggedy shapes, rags-and-tatters, with a little pasta-cutting wheel or a blunt-edged knife. Toss the scraps with a very little semolina and drop them into piles on the board, keeping your fingers light and airy so that the scraps don't stick to each other. Repeat with the other 3 balls. Let the scraps rest for another 10 minutes.

Now set aside a handful of the pasta scraps to fry as a crisp topping. Drop a pat of butter into a serving bowl and set it aside to warm ready for the cooked pasta. Bring a large pot of water to a boil—pasta needs lots of room. Drop in the rags-and-tatters a few at a time so that the water never stops bubbling. Give the pot a quick stir to separate the pasta scraps and cook until they bob to the surface—2–3 minutes, depending upon their thickness. Remove them with a slotted spoon and toss them in the butter in the warm serving bowl.

Meanwhile, fry the reserved raw pasta scraps in a little oil until they're crisp and puffy. Toss the pasta with the crushed toasted hazelnuts and top with the crispy pasta, a trickle of honey, and a spoonful of yogurt.

fattoush
Middle Eastern bread salad

A lemony Mediterranean bread salad, flavored with lots of fresh herbs—easy and great fun to make. The dressing includes sumac, a particularly Middle Eastern flavoring made from dried berries which have a deliciously sharp, lemony flavor.

Split the pita breads down the middle—not necessary if you're using bread—and toast them. Tear them into bite-sized pieces and drop into a salad bowl. Sprinkle with the sumac (or lemon zest) and the olive oil, and mix together delicately with your hands.

Now prepare the herbs: pick them over and remove any dirt with your fingers, rinsing them only if it's really necessary and drying them carefully. Strip the leaves from the tougher stalks.

When you're ready to eat, toss the rest of the ingredients with the bread in the bowl, adding the tomatoes, cucumbers, and scallions first, and the herbs last. Dress with about 2 tablespoons lemon juice and a little sea salt.

**Serves 2 children and
2 adults**

4 small pita breads or 4 thick
  slices day-old country bread
1 tablespoon sumac (or finely
  grated lemon zest)
¼ cup olive oil
2 handfuls of flat-leaf parsley
1 handful of purslane (or chervil
  or extra parsley)
½ handful of fresh mint
6 small, ripe tomatoes, quartered
1–2 small cucumber(s), chopped
2–3 scallions, trimmed and
  chopped
juice of 1–2 lemon(s)
sea salt

You need a knife, a
salad bowl, and a toaster.

spinach and cheese phyllo turnovers
boreki

Crisp little triangular turnovers of phyllo pastry dough, fiddly to make but very good if the filling is as delicious as it should be. Spinach and curd cheese are one of the two classic combinations popular in Turkey, the other being ground meat cooked with onion and spices.

Cut the pastry dough into strips as wide as your hand—don't unroll it first; you need the full length of the dough—and keep it covered with plastic wrap while you work so it doesn't dry out.

To make the filling, mash the spinach, cheeses, and cinnamon together to make a soft paste, seasoning with pepper and a little salt (not too much as the cheeses are already salty).

Put a teaspoon of the filling on the short edge of the first strip. Fold the strip diagonally over the filling to make a triangle, then fold it again to make another triangle—just remember you need to place the cut edge against the cut edge on the opposite side. Continue until you've used up the whole strip and you have a neat little package. Seal the last fold with a drop of water from a wet finger and transfer to a baking sheet that's been brushed with melted butter or oil. Repeat until all are done, leaving a little space between each or they'll stick to one another. Never mind if they look a bit messy, just as long the filling is well wrapped. You can vary the shape by rolling the packages up like little cigars—don't forget to tuck the sides in halfway through to enclose the filling.

To bake, preheat the oven to 350°F. Brush the tops of the boreki with melted butter and bake for 10 minutes, until well puffed and golden. Alternatively, to fry, heat enough oil in a frying pan to submerge the boreki. When the oil is lightly hazed with blue, fry them a few at a time, turning once, until the pastry is crisp and brown, then transfer to paper towels to drain. Let cool a little before eating.

Makes about 24

half a 1-pound package
  phyllo dough
9 ounces cooked, well-drained
  spinach, squeezed dry
4 ounces soft white curd cheese
  (labna or ricotta)
2 ounces hard cheese (cheddar
  or Gruyère), grated
1 teaspoon ground cinnamon
salt and pepper

For finishing
2 tablespoons melted butter
  for brushing, or oil for
  shallow-frying

You need a knife, a mixing bowl, a fork, plastic wrap, a teaspoon and a pastry brush and either a baking sheet or a frying pan. This recipe uses the oven or the top of the stove.

pull-aparts

Bread rolls baked close together so the sides are soft and white when you pull one from the other are perfect for sharing with friends because you don't tear them apart until you want to eat them.

Makes about 18

18 ounces white bread
flour (unbleached)
½ teaspoon salt
one ⅗-ounce cube fresh
compressed yeast or 1 teaspoon
dry yeast (or follow the
measurements on the package)
¼ cup (½ stick) butter
about 1¼ cups warm milk
1 egg, whisked with a fork to blend

You need a mixing bowl and sifter, a cup and spoon, a plastic bag and a roasting pan or a baking sheet with a deep lip. This recipe uses the oven.

Before you begin, set everything out on the table including the mixing bowl and let it warm in the heat of the kitchen. Sift the flour and salt into the mixing bowl. If using fresh yeast, mix it with a little warm water and a pinch of sugar to start it working quickly. If using dry or instant yeast, mix it straight into the flour, or follow the instructions on the package. Chop the butter into little pieces and drop it into the warm milk, which should be just hot enough to melt the butter.

Use your fist to make a well in the middle of the flour. Pour in the bubbly yeast mixture, if using fresh yeast, and the egg. Stirring with your hand, work in enough of the warm, buttery milk to make a soft, sticky dough. Tip it out onto a clean counter or wooden board dusted with a little flour (don't bother to clean your hands: the stickiness will come off as you work). Knead the dough with your fists, pushing and pulling until it forms itself into a smooth ball and your hands are no longer sticky.

Drop the dough ball back into the bowl and pop the whole thing into a plastic bag. Tie the bag loosely and put it in a warm place for 1 hour for the yeast to work and the dough to become light and puffy; it's ready when it keeps the mark of your finger when you prod it. Knead it again to knock the bubbles out, and work the dough into a rope. Chop the rope into 18 little pieces. Drop each piece one by one into your cupped hand and form it gently into a neat, smooth ball. Arrange the dough balls in a buttered roasting pan or on a baking sheet with a deep lip, setting them about a finger's width apart. Cover with the plastic bag again and let rise for another 40 minutes.

Preheat the oven to 425°F.

Bake the rolls for 30–35 minutes, until well risen and golden brown.

blueberry corn-muffins

Sunny golden muffins to bake for a Sunday breakfast party—never mind if they look a bit lop-sided, they'll still taste delicious.

Preheat the oven to 400°F and warm the milk and butter in a small pan until the butter melts.

Meanwhile, butter a 12-hole muffin pan—the holes are deeper than the ones used for cupcakes, and you need plenty of depth so that the muffins can puff up like little chef's hats.

Sift the flour with the baking powder into a bowl and mix in the cornmeal, sugar, and a pinch of salt. Make a well in the middle with your fist. When the buttery milk has cooled to finger heat, pour it into the hollow in the flour mixture. Tip the egg into the milk and stir everything together until well blended and free of lumps. Fold in the blueberries.

Spoon the mixture into the buttered muffin pan—it should come about two thirds of the way up each hole.

Bake the muffins for 20–25 minutes until they're well risen and the tops are golden brown. Transfer to a wire rack to cool.

Makes about 12

1 cup milk
½ cup plus 1 tablespoon butter, roughly chopped
4½ ounces all-purpose flour
2 teaspoons baking powder
9 ounces fine-ground cornmeal
2 tablespoons sugar
salt
1 organic cage-free egg, whisked with a fork to blend
2 heaping tablespoons fresh blueberries

You need a small saucepan, a muffin pan with 12 deep holes, a mixing bowl and sifter, a wooden spoon, a small bowl and fork and a metal spoon. This recipe uses both the stovetop and the oven.

cupcakes

Makes about 12

¾ cup unsalted butter, softened
¾ cup sugar
6 ounces all-purpose flour
1 teaspoon baking powder
3 medium organic cage-free eggs

For finishing
about 4 tablespoons
confectioners' sugar
candy sprinkles

You need 2 mixing bowls, a sieve, a wooden spoon and a metal spoon, about 12 cupcake cases and a baking sheet. We used heatproof cupcake cases which don't collapse. Paper ones can be supported by dropping them in a 12-hole tart tin. This recipe uses the oven.

First-time cooks can whip up a cake "batter" with dry rice and lentils plus a few candy sprinkles for fun, and then help decorate the real cakes when they're baked. Older and more experienced kitchen-collaborators can do it all without any help.

Put the softened butter in a warm mixing bowl along with the sugar and beat it with a wooden spoon until it's really light and pale. Or use an electric beater.

Sift the flour with the baking powder into another bowl.

Crack the eggs into a cup, one at a time, and beat each egg into the butter and sugar, still using the wooden spoon and adding a little flour if the mixture looks like splitting. Change spoons: you need a metal one for the next step. Mix in the rest of the flour carefully, adding it spoonful by spoonful and turning the mixture over and over to blend it thoroughly—there should be no little pockets of white flour when you've finished.

Preheat the oven to 375°F. Meanwhile, arrange 12 cupcake cups on a baking sheet. Spoon the batter into the cups carefully—don't fill them right to the top.

Bake for 25–30 minutes—check after 20 minutes—until well risen, brown, and firm. Use your nose and your ears when the oven's open: the cakes will smell all buttery and delicious, and when they're ready, they stop hissing.

Let the cakes cool in their paper cups and frost them as soon as they're cool. Mix the confectioners' sugar with enough cold water to make a trickling cream of an icing. A few candy sprinkles will finish the cakes off nicely.

Frances says: The first job I ever had was making my dad's packed lunch every day. I decided what to make, shopped for what I needed, kept to a budget, and at the end of the week, he paid me my wages and told me how much he liked what I'd cooked—which taught me how important it is for children to have something good to take to school. So here are 12 great lunchbox recipes—wraps, fistfuls, cakes, and cookies—plus a tasty after-school snack.

off to school

Elisabeth says: Packed lunches mean different things in different parts of the world: all they have in common is that they must be easy to carry and taste good even when they've cooled. In great-granny's day, when all country children walked to school, everyone knew which wild leaves, berries, and nuts could be nibbled along the way, adding a healthy dose of fresh greens and fruit to the day's intake, plus the exercise that came with the territory.

9

asparagus and potato tortilla

tortilla de asparagos trigueros

In Spain, a packed lunch usually includes a wedge of Spanish omelet, a firm, juicy egg-cake in which potato provides the bulk. This version includes a few spears of fresh green asparagus, though you can leave it plain or include anything else you fancy that will add interest. The only rule is that all additions must be fully cooked before they're mixed with the egg. Other favorite extras are green beans, slivered artichoke hearts, chopped red peppers, cubes of serrano ham or chorizo.

Chop the asparagus into bite-sized pieces. Peel and cube the potatoes, or cut them into thin slivers or fries. Crack the eggs into a bowl and fork them up with the salt—they should be well blended but not frothy. The volume of the additions should equal that of the egg: when you've prepared the vegetables, measure roughly by eye.

In a small frying pan, heat enough oil to submerge the potatoes completely—a French omelet pan is just the right size and shape. As soon as the oil is lightly hazed with blue, add the potatoes and fry them gently until soft—don't let them brown—then transfer with a slotted spoon to a strainer set over a bowl to catch the drippings. Fry the asparagus pieces for no more than a minute—just enough to heat them through. Transfer the asparagus to the strainer holding the potato and then tip everything, including the oil drippings, into the egg, turning to blend.

Tip out all but 1 tablespoon of oil from the pan. Reheat the pan and pour in the egg mixture. Cook gently—high heat makes eggs leathery—lifting the edges to allow the uncooked egg to run underneath. You can speed up the egg-setting process by placing a lid on the pan. When the egg begins to look set in the middle—3–4 minutes—shake the pan to make sure the tortilla base is loose.

Remove from the heat. Now, with the handle in one hand and a plate in the other, place the plate over the pan, face-side down, and tip the whole thing upside-down in one quick movement. Replace the pan on the heat, add a little more oil, and slip the tortilla into the pan, this time with the soft side downwards. Be brave—it's easy; if you're nervous at first, put a cloth over your arm to protect you from oily drips. Cook the other side for another 2–3 minutes, neatening the sides with a spatula to build up a firm edge. The middle should still be juicy and the outside perfectly firm. Tip the tortilla out onto paper towels, pat off the excess oil, let it cool to room temperature, and cut into neat quarters or squares.

Serves 4 children

4–5 thin green asparagus spears, trimmed
2 large potatoes
3 large organic cage-free eggs
½ teaspoon salt
oil for frying

For balance, sliced oranges and bread—no Spaniard would dream of a meal without bread.

Indonesian coconut rice rolls
lempur

In tropical regions where the heat is fierce during the day, children attend school from early morning until it's time for the noontime meal, having a snack to bridge the gap. In its simplest form, this is a helping of coconut rice with a little flavouring dip of spices and dried powdered shrimp (*blacan*) to be mixed in with the fingers. In the old days the wrapping was a banana leaf, replaced in modern times by a plastic box, depriving children, say those who remember their own schooldays, of the subtle flavor of the leaves as well as the pleasure of unwrapping the package. If you can't find banana leaves, use baking foil or baking parchment.

Put the rice in a heavy saucepan with the coconut milk and salt, bring to a boil, turn the heat right down, tightly cover, and cook very gently for 20 minutes, until the rice is tender and the liquid has all been absorbed. If it still looks damp, stir around the edges with a fork, and cook uncovered for another 5 minutes. Set aside to cool.

You're now ready to assemble the wraps.

Preheat the oven to 350°F.

Cut a sheet of baking foil or parchment into rectangles about the length and width of your hand. Lay the squares on the table and brush the middle of each square with a little oil.

Lay 1 heaped tablespoon of the rice on each wrapper, using the back of the spoon to make a dip in the middle. Place a piece of avocado, a sprinkle of lime juice, a scrap of ginger, and a sprig of cilantro in each dip, and mold the rice over the filling to form a little cylinder. Fold the wrapper over the cylinder, tucking in the sides halfway through the rolling to make a neat little wrapped packages.

Transfer the wraps to a baking sheet and bake for 15 minutes until heated through—test with your finger—to allow the rice to take on the flavor of the filling. Remove and let cool to room temperature.

Makes 12

For the rice
2 cups glutinous rice (*ketan*) or any short-grain rice
4 cups coconut milk
½ teaspoon salt
oil for brushing

For the filling
1 firm avocado, cut into sticks
juice of 1 lime
1 small slice fresh ginger root, cut into matchsticks
12 small sprigs of cilantro

For balance, toasted shredded coconut and chunks of papaya.

slow-cooked beef with wine and olives
daube de boeuf provençale

Thermos food—something soupy and spoonable which keeps its heat without drying out—is a good way to provide a hot meal to eat at school on a cold day. The traditional French daube is a robust beef stew cooked with the rough red wine of Provence—no need to worry about the alcohol as it evaporates during the first few minutes of cooking, leaving the wine to deepen the flavor and help to tenderize the meat.

A daube was the traditional Sunday dinner in the cold uplands of the Languedoc where my children attended school some 30 years ago. The youngest was at the local nursery school—école maternelle. She took her lunch in a canteen, an enamel bucket with a sealable lid. In the bottom was a ladleful of daube or some other soupy stew and on the top was a little metal dish for the hors d'oeuvre: olives, celeriac in mustardy mayonnaise, grated carrot, a little tomato salad. The school lunch lady collected all the canteens as the children arrived, removed the hors d'oeuvres, and set them at each child's place, then resealed the containers and popped them in a big pot of boiling water to heat up for the lunch break. The school provided fresh bread and water, and everyone ate heartily and well.

Drop the meat into a plastic or paper bag with the seasoned flour and shake to coat. Heat the oil in a large heavy pan. Add the meat and toss it over the heat for 4–5 minutes till it browns a little on all sides. Remove and reserve. Add the bacon, shallots or onions, and carrot to the pan, and fry till everything sizzles and takes a little color. Return the meat to the pan and add the olives, orange zest, cinnamon, crushed peppercorns, thyme, and bay. Add the red wine and enough water to submerge the meat—about 2 cups—and let it bubble it up, stirring to avoid sticking, till the steam no longer smells of alcohol.

Turn down the heat, cover the pot securely (seal it with a flour-and-water paste if the fit isn't perfect), and either simmer very gently over a low heat or transfer to a medium oven, 325°F. Cook for 1½–2 hours till the meat is so tender it can be eaten with a spoon. You may need to add a little more water towards the end of cooking, to prevent it drying out. Check the seasoning— you may want a little sugar to balance the acidity of the wine, but you shouldn't need extra salt as the bacon and olives provide plenty.

Serves 12 children and
2 adults

2¼ pounds stewing beef, trimmed
  and cut up
1 tablespoon seasoned flour
2 tablespoons olive oil
2 tablespoons chopped bacon
  (include the rind)
18 ounces shallots or baby
  onions, peeled
4 garlic cloves, skinned and
  crushed
1 large carrot, scraped and chopped
1 tablespoon black olives
2–3 curls dried orange zest
  (see below)
1 short piece cinnamon stick
½ teaspoon crushed peppercorns
1 sprig of thyme
1–2 bay leaves
2 cups young red wine
  (nothing grand)
salt and pepper

For balance, a hunk of fresh baguette and a little carton of fruit-flavored yogurt.

To prepare your own dried orange zest, peel the zest from a large orange and set it to dry for a week or two in the sun on a windowsill.

meatballs in bulgur
kibbeh

Spiced ground meat enclosed in a thin shell of bulgur, Lebanon's favorite finger food takes time, patience, and a great deal of skill. This somewhat rough-and-ready version from the Dominican Republic (blame an influx of Lebanese immigrants) is quick and it works.

Put the bulgur in a bowl and pour in enough boiling water to cover the grains to a depth of one finger. Stir and let it swell for 1 hour.

Meanwhile, fry the meat with the onion—you may need a little oil—until all the juices have evaporated and the meat begins to brown. Sprinkle in the parsley and cinnamon and season with the salt and pepper. Turn well to blend, remove from the heat, and set aside to cool.

When the bulgur has absorbed all the moisture, mix half into the meat mixture and work it with your hands or in a food processor until it's firm enough to hold together. Have a bowl of warm water by your side to dampen your hands and work the mixture into 12 small, torpedo-shaped balls. Roll the balls in the remaining bulgur, pressing to coat. Transfer to a baking sheet lined with plastic wrap. Repeat until all the ingredients are used up and you have neat little rows of torpedoes, each just enough for two bites. Let it set for 30 minutes, or overnight in the fridge.

In a frying pan, heat enough oil to submerge the kibbeh. When the oil smokes a little, slip them in—not too many at a time—and fry, turning carefully, until perfectly golden and crisp, about 6–7 minutes. Transfer to paper towels to drain.

Makes 12

**9 ounces fine bulgur
(cracked wheat)**

For the filling
18 ounces ground lamb
oil for frying
1 medium onion, peeled and grated
1 tablespoon chopped parsley
1 teaspoon ground cinnamon
1 teaspoon salt
½ teaspoon pepper

For balance, cucumber sticks and fresh or dried apricots, with a handful of almonds for nibbling.

ham and tomato pasties

pastelitos de jamón

Makes 12

For the filling

2 tablespoons olive oil
1 onion, peeled and finely chopped
1 garlic clove, skinned and crushed
18 ounces ripe tomatoes, skinned, seeded and chopped
1 teaspoon oregano
4 ounces ham or lean bacon, chopped
9 ounces chopped pumpkin or chayote

For the pastry dough

12 ounces white bread flour
1 teaspoon baking powder
½ teaspoon salt
¼ cup oil
¼ cup milk
about ⅔ cup boiling water

For balance, tropical fruit: pineapple chunks or the small, sweet, juicy Windward Isles bananas.

The mid-morning snack—*merienda*—a child takes to school in a tropical climate such as that of the Caribbean needs to be something which won't become inedible in the heat. Salt-cured pork products such as ham and chorizo fit the bill because the method of curing ensures that the meat has no need of refrigeration.

To make the filling, heat the oil in a frying pan and gently fry the onion and garlic until they soften—3–4 minutes. Add the chopped tomatoes and oregano and a spoonful of cold water, let it bubble up again, reduce the heat, and cook gently for 5–10 minutes, mashing with a wooden spoon, until the tomatoes collapse and the sauce thickens. Stir in the ham or bacon and the diced pumpkin or chayote and bubble up again until the vegetable softens. Remove the pan from the heat and set aside to cool while you mix the pastry dough. A hot-water crust pastry dough has to be used while it's still warm—no resting time required.

Preheat the oven to 400°F.

Sift the flour, baking powder, and salt into a bowl and make a well in the middle. In a measuring cup, mix the oil and milk with the boiling water and pour it into the well. Work the dry and wet ingredients together until you have a soft, sticky dough. Knead it until smooth and elastic; don't take too long, as the dough should be worked while it's warm. Form it into a roll and chop it into 12 equal pieces. Roll out each piece into a thin disc with a lightly floured rolling pin, or pat them out between 2 sheets of plastic wrap. Put a teaspoon of the filling into the center of each disc. Wet the edges with a damp finger and fold one half over the other to enclose the filling. Mark the edges with a fork to seal. Transfer the pasties to an oiled baking sheet.

Bake for about 15 minutes, until the pastry is golden and crisp. Transfer to a wire rack to cool.

Cornish pasties

Makes 4 child-sized pasties

For the pastry dough
12 ounces white bread flour
½ teaspoon salt
⅓ cup lard, frozen
⅓ cup butter, frozen
4–5 tablespoons cold water

For the filling
4 ounces onion, peeled and sliced
into fine half moons
9 ounces turnip, peeled and
cut into matchsticks
12 ounces lean beef, slivered
across the grain
18 ounces potatoes, peeled and
cut into matchsticks
salt and pepper

For balance, a crisp apple
or a well-scrubbed carrot.

Cold-water pastry like
this must be kept cold
throughout its preparation of
it'll be heavy. A hot-water
pastry, like that used for the
Caribbean ham and tomato
pasties on the previous page,
must not be allowed to cool
or it'll crumble and collapse.

The Cornish tin-miner's traditional lunch break was also tucked in the pocket of Cornish schoolchildren in the days when everyone walked to school. The size of the pasty depends on the size of the person, but one pasty should be enough to satisfy the pangs of hunger all day. It was the custom to mark each pasty with an initial, so that there was no mistaking which one was yours.

Make the pastry first. Everything should be as cold as possible. Sift the flour with the salt into a bowl and leave it in the fridge for 1–2 hours.

When the flour is really cold, grate in the fat and stir it in with a knife. Mix in enough cold water to make a manageable dough. Knead it for a moment, but not for long. The fat should remain quite lumpy, to give a firm enough crust to hold the juices of the filling. Cover the dough ball with plastic wrap and leave it in the fridge for at least 30 minutes.

Preheat the oven to 400°F.

Divide the dough into 4 equal pieces and roll each piece out on a floured board into discs the size of a saucer. Drop a little onion into the middle of each disc, top with a layer of turnip, then with meat, then with potato, seasoning as you go and making sure the filling will reach right into the ends when you make your turnovers.

Dampen the pastry dough edges with a wet finger, then bring the sides together over the top to form a fat bolster. Pinch the edges together firmly, starting at the middle and finishing at the corners. Dry your fingers, then crimp the pinched edge between your thumb and forefinger to form a rope—the seal needs to be perfect. Transfer the pasties to a non-stick baking sheet; don't prick or slit them.

Bake for 15 minutes in the hot oven to crisp and brown the crust, then turn the oven down to 350°F, lay a sheet of foil on top of the pasties, shiny side down, and continue baking for another 25 minutes to cook the insides.

If you're baking them in the morning, they can be cooked while the family eats breakfast. Pop each pasty into its own paper bag and it'll stay warm until the lunch break comes.

oatcakes with cream crowdie

Fine-ground oatmeal, also known as steel-cut oats, gives a smooth, crisp Scottish oatcake to eat with cream cheese—crowdie. Make sure you have proper milled oatmeal—rolled oats won't do.

Preheat the oven to 300°F or set a griddle to heat.

In a roomy bowl, mix the oatmeal with the salt. Mash in the fat—drippings, lard, or butter—with a fork or your fingers. Work in enough warm water to make a firm dough. Form it into a ball and pat it out between 2 sheets of plastic wrap until it's about 1/8-inch thick. Cut into circles with a sharp-edged wine glass or cookie cutter.

If you're using the oven, transfer the oatcakes to a lightly greased baking sheet, and bake for 30–40 minutes, until the oatcakes look dry and crisp and a little brown at the edges; don't let them take color all over. Transfer carefully to a wire rack and let cool.

If you're using a griddle, wipe it over with a scrap of clean cloth dipped in drippings or butter, and test the heat with a sprinkle of flour: the grains should turn golden by the time you've counted to ten. Transfer the oatcakes to the hot surface and bake gently until dry and lightly browned at the edges. Stack the oatcakes in a rack in front of the heat to dry them off completely.

Store them buried in a jar of steel-cut oats, or wrapped in a clean cloth in a tin. If the oatcakes soften in storage, warm them up again in a gentle oven: they'll crisp as they cool. Take them to school as a mid-morning snack to eat with the crowdie—a piece for the pocket, as they say in Scotland.

Makes about 24 oatcakes

18 ounces fine-ground oatmeal
   (steel-cut oats)
½ teaspoon salt
2 tablespoons drippings or
   lard or butter
about 1¼ cups warm water

For serving
2 ounces cream cheese per person

For balance, a carton of fresh raspberries or a crunchy apple.

cut-and-come-again cake

Makes a 3-pound cake

For the first cooking:
1¼ cups currants
1¼ cups raisins
½ cup brown sugar
2 tablespoons vinegar
2 tablespoons water

For the second cooking:
18 ounces all-purpose flour
2 teaspoons baking powder
¼ cup sugar
½ cup (1 stick) butter
7 fl. oz. (a scant cup) buttermilk

For balance, cheddar cheese
and a Cox's Orange Pippin.

An old-fashioned English nursery recipe, this'll keep for months in a tin, which is why it got its name. The cake batter is cooked twice—first boiled, then baked.

Put the first-cooking ingredients into a small pan. Stir; transfer to the heat, and simmer gently for 10 minutes, stirring occasionally, then remove and leave aside to cool.

Preheat the oven to 400°F.

Meanwhile, sift the flour and baking powder into a bowl and mix in the sugar. Rub in the butter until the mixture is like fine bread crumbs. Stir in enough buttermilk to give a firm batter. Fold in the cooled fruit mixture.

Pour the batter into a 9 x 5 x 3-inch loaf tin lined with baking parchment.

Bake in the hot oven for 20 minutes, then reduce the heat to 325°F and bake for another 30–40 minutes, until the cake is well risen and firm; keep an eye on it and cover it with foil (shiny side upwards, to deflect the heat) if the top browns too fast. Transfer to a wire rack to cool. Remove the paper before you store it in a tin.

Welshcakes

Halfway between cookies and biscuits, these are the treat at the bottom of a Welsh schoolchild's lunchbox. They're easy to make and even easier to eat.

Rub the butter into the flour and add the raisins and sugar. Mix the water with the eggs and add to the dry ingredients to make a soft dough. Tip onto a well-floured board or counter and roll it out to a thickness of $1/2$ inch. Cut into circles with a sharp-edged water glass or a $2^1/2$-inch cookie cutter.

Heat the griddle or a heavy frying pan gently and thoroughly—don't let it overheat.

Slip the cakes onto the hot metal and wait until the underside browns and the top begins to dry—about 4–5 minutes. Turn gently to cook the other side. Transfer to a clean cloth to cool. Store in an airtight tin.

Makes 24

2 tablespoons butter
18 ounces self-rising flour
2 tablespoons raisins
½ cup sugar
7 fl. oz. water
2 large organic cage-free eggs

For balance,
vegetable soup in
a thermos.

paradise cookies
croquantes de granos de paraíso

These crisp little cookies pack an unusual punch since they include amaranth seeds, an important food source for the Aztecs. Modern Mexicans know them as *granos de paraíso*, seeds of paradise, and include them in nut brittles as well as in crisp buttery cookies. They are sold as after-school snacks at dozens of road-side kiosks, along with a paper cone of fresh fruit prepared to order and offered with a shake of chili powder instead of sugar.

Makes about 24

5½ ounces all-purpose flour
2 tablespoons amaranth seeds
½ cup butter
¼ cup sugar

For finishing
walnut or pecan halves

For balance, tropical fruit: chunks of watermelon for the juiciness you need in a hot climate, passion fruit for portability and the excitement of biting into the leathery skin and sucking out the pulp.

Sift the flour into a mixing bowl and mix in the amaranth seeds. Beat the butter with the sugar until light and pale. Using the tips of your fingers, work in enough of the flour mixture to make a soft dough—stop before it goes crumbly. Press the dough lightly into a ball, still using the tips of your fingers, and roll it in plastic wrap. Set in a cool place to rest for 20–30 minutes for the seeds and flour to swell.

Preheat the oven to 300°F.

Dust a board or clean counter with a little flour. Unwrap the dough ball and put the plastic wrap to one side. Drop the dough ball onto the floured surface and flatten it to make a thick disc, then re-wrap the dough in the plastic. Roll or pat out to the thickness of your thumb. Remove the plastic wrap and cut out small discs with a cookie cutter and transfer to a buttered baking sheet lightly dusted with flour. Gather the scraps together, pat out again, stamp out more circles until the dough is all used up. Make a dent in the top of each cookie with a damp finger and press in a half walnut or pecan.

Bake for 30–40 minutes. The cookies will spread as they cook—don't worry, just let 'em wander. Remove when they're nicely browned at the edges; they'll crisp as they cool. Transfer to a wire rack as soon as they harden a little, and let cool completely before you break them into convenient pieces. They keep well in an airtight tin.

honey and almond shortbreads
kourabiedes

Olive oil is used instead of butter in these nutty little cinnamon-flavored cookies—nuts provide the protein, honey serves as the sweetener. Well, nobody's perfect.

Makes about 24

8 ounces all-purpose flour
I teaspoon ground cinnamon
4 ounces ground almonds
I teaspoon finely grated
orange zest
I cup light olive oil
⅓ cup runny honey
I organic cage-free egg,
whisked with a fork to blend

For balance, olives and cheese: kefalotiri and feta are good and Greek.

Sift the flour with the cinnamon into a roomy bowl, then mix in the ground almonds and the orange zest.

Beat the olive oil with the honey until well blended, then beat it into the flour, adding enough egg to form a ball of soft dough which just holds its shape—you may need to use less egg or add a little water. Or drop everything into a food processor and run it until the dough forms into a single lump.

Cover the dough with plastic wrap and let it rest and firm in the fridge for 1 hour.

Preheat the oven to 425°F.

On a lightly floured board or counter, roll the dough out to the thickness of your little finger. Using a cookie cutter, cut out bite-sized circles and transfer them to a buttered, lightly floured baking sheet. Press the scraps together with your fingertips to form a ball, pat that out, and cut out more circles, and repeat until all the dough is used up.

Bake the shortbreads for 15–20 minutes until they're pale gold and perfectly dry. Lift them carefully onto a wire rack to cool and crisp. Store in an airtight tin.

Swedish butter-cookies
smörkaker

Little ring-shaped cookies spiced with cardamom, a popular flavoring for sweet things in Scandinavia. Cardamom flavors the Christmas dessert, a creamy rice pudding, and is included in the spice-mix for gingerbread, *pepperkaker*.

Beat the butter with the sugar until fluffy and pale. Beat in the lemon juice and zest. Sift in the flour, add the cardamom, and beat with a wooden spoon until you have a smooth soft dough—you'll probably need a spoonful or two of cold water. Or do the whole thing in a food processor.

Form the dough into a ball, cover with plastic wrap, and set it in the fridge for 1–2 hours to rest and firm up. Turn the dough ball out onto a lightly floured pastry board or counter, flatten it with little pats of the rolling pin, and roll it out into a long rectangle about 12 x 4 inches. Cut it into 4-inch-long strips about as wide as your little finger.

Preheat the oven to 350°F.

Twist 2 of the pastry strips together and join them into a ring with a dampened finger. Continue until all the strips are formed into pairs and rings. Arrange on a well-buttered baking sheet and bake for about 10 minutes until golden. Transfer to a wire rack to cool. Store in an airtight tin.

Makes about 30

1¾ cup unsalted butter, softened
1½ cups sugar
juice and finely grated zest
    of 1 lemon
17 ounces all-purpose flour
1 teaspoon crushed
    cardamom seeds

For balance, pea soup in a thermos.

crêpe soup

frittensuppe

Serves 2 children and 2 adults

4 cups strong beef stock
(see right)

For the pancakes
3 organic cage-free eggs
9 ounces flour
about 1 cup milk
salt
grated nutmeg
butter for frying

For finishing
chopped parsley or chives

*For 1 quart of beef
stock*—enough for 2 children
and 2 adults—you need
4 segments of sawn-up marrow
bones. Roast in a hot oven,
transfer to a large pot and add a
handful of chopped root vegetables—parsley root, carrot,
onion, leek—and a few allspice
berries. Add enough water to
cover generously and simmer
for at least an hour. In a
pressure cooker, 10 minutes is
all it needs. Strain, discarding the
solids, and bubble up till
reduced to 1 quart.

There's nothing like a steaming bowl of soup as a pick-me-up after a long day in a cold schoolroom. Austrian children count themselves lucky to come home to a bowl of *frittensuppe*, clear beef-bone stock with crêpe ribbons added in much the same way as noodles. Parsley is the only additional flavoring. Serve all three elements separately for freedom of choice.

For 1 quart of beef broth – enough for 2 children and 2 adults – you need 4 segments of sawn-up marrow bones. Beef shin or osso bucco can replace the marrow bones – allow 1 pound, tied in a piece. Roast in a hot oven, transfer to a large boiling pot and add a handful of diced root vegetables – parsley root, carrot, onion, leek – and a few allspice berries. Add enough water to cover generously and simmer for at least an hour. In a pressure cooker, 10 minutes is all it needs. Strain, discarding the solids, and bubble up until it is reduced to 1 quart. Don't skim off all the little globules of golden fat: they add richness and confirm that the broth is home-made.

Heat the stock while you make the crêpes. Whisk the eggs, flour, and milk thoroughly together in a large measuring cup until you have a smooth, pourable cream, and season with a little salt and nutmeg. Or put everything in a food processor or blender, and whizz to a creamy consistancy.

Melt a nugget of butter in a crêpe pan—a small frying pan with a very smooth surface. As soon as the butter froths, pour in a little of the batter, just enough to coat the bottom of the pan, and swirl it around to spread the mixture evenly. When the crêpe's dry on top, it's ready to turn. Flip it over and cook the other side. Repeat until all the batter is used up. Pile up the crêpes in a clean cloth as you go. When all the crêpes are cooked, cut the pile right through in quarters, and slice the quarters into fine strips like tagliatelle.

Ladle the stock into soup bowls and finish each portion with crêpe strips and a sprinkle of parsley or chives.

index

acknowledgements

Elisabeth says: I owe a long-standing debt of gratitude to my own children, Caspar, Francesca, Poppy, and Honey, who were the initial recipients of my enthusiasm for taking the youngest members of the household on exotic gastronomic tours—even if the journey was only in the mind.

To my grandchildren—seven at the last count—the dedicatees of this book, who have had to put up with much culinary experimentation while the book was in preparation.

To friends and colleagues—food-writers or child-carers (sometimes both)—for their willingness to share their knowledge.

To my agent, Abner Stein, without whom I wouldn't be a writer.

To editor Caroline Taggart for unfailing support and enthusiasm.

To designer Jenny Semple for tolerance and patience with the various artistic temperaments involved in the planning stages.

And to my daughter-in-law and co-author, for her love and the pleasure we take in working together.

Frances says: I am thankful to Vanessa Holden for her quick design concepts—she's a genius.

To Ayesha Patel for introducing me to the joys of prop-rental companies, for her keen eye and sweet modern sensibility.

To Ngoc for taking such beautiful pictures, and her patience, energy and willingness to drink lukewarm tea.

To my mother-in-law for persevering with this project and for birthing her son, my husband—my love.

To Evelyn Rosario and Ziola Hidalgo for taking such good care of Sophie and Plum—for all their love and patience and for introducing the girls to La Comida and the joys of red beans and rice.

And to all our precious models, the children who have come to make this world a better place.